Instructor's Guide to Accompany

C by Dissection
The Essentials of C Programming
SECOND EDITION

KELLEY • POHL

James C. Munyer
UNIVERSITY OF CALIFORNIA

The Benjamin/Cummings Publishing Company, Inc.
Redwood City, California • Menlo Park, California • Reading, Massachusetts
New York • Don Mills, Ontario • Wokingham, U.K. • Amsterdam •Bonn
Sydney • Singapore • Tokyo • Madrid • San Juan

ISBN 0-8053-3141-7

12345678910-BK-95 94 93 92

The Benjamin/Cummings Publishing Company, Inc.
390 Bridge Parkway
Redwood City, California 94065

Preface

Introductory programming in C has been taught here at the University of California at Santa Cruz for several years using the first edition of *C By Dissection*, and the authors' other text, *A Book On C*. The course has generally been successful in teaching C to both non-computer science majors with little or no previous programming experience, and CIS majors who already know one other language.

Answers are provided for nearly every exercise in the text, the only exceptions being a few exercises which do not really call for an answer, such as where a fragment of code is supplied to the student to type in and compile. Answers to exercises which involved writing C program code, or which asked for the output of a given program, were verified by compiling and running the relevant code using the Free Software Foundation Gnu ANSI C compiler (otherwise known as "gcc") running on a VAX computer. Solutions for chapter 16, involving C++ code, were verified with a C++ to C preprocessor and an ANSI C compiler. Solutions involving program code are also available on a solutions diskette.

In many cases, the exercises build on examples from the text and on each other; therefore many solutions use functions already presented. In this Instructor's Guide these common functions are not repeated each time they are used, in order to save space, but are referenced via function prototypes. In the diskette, however, each solution is a complete program in itself. (Normally common functions would be separately compiled modules, but in the large and diverse collection of software on the disk, it was felt that this approach would cause confusion.)

Two programming projects are also supplied for most of the chapters. These are intended to simulate "real world" programming tasks, to make use of significant topics from the chapter, and also to be interesting to the student. Here at U.C.S.C., where the course is taught in a 10-week format, they are given out as weekly programming assignments. The students find them challenging but "do-able". I like to put an executable version of my own solution to the project on-line and publically accessible so that students can experiment with it and verify their understanding of the problem. Teaching assistants should be encouraged to give hints to students who are having trouble getting started with the projects. Solutions to each programming project, and test data where appropriate, are also provided on the solutions diskette.

James Curie Munyer
University of California at Santa Cruz
November, 1991

Table of Contents

Transparency Masters

CHAPTER 1

WRITING AN ANSI C PROGRAM

The first chapter of *C By Dissection* gives a general overview of the ANSI C language. The important points to cover are:

- The programming process: analysis, coding, text editor, compiler, program execution, debugging.

- The basic format of a C program: preprocessor commands, `main()`, and sequential statement execution.

- Statements for input and output: `printf` and `scanf`.

- The concept of variables, variable declarations, and assignments.

With these concepts the student should be able to start writing simple programs right away. Another point which should be covered at the beginning of the course, but which for obvious reasons is not covered in detail in the text, is

- Using the operating system at your particular site, how to use the text editor, and how to run the compiler.

Chapter 1 also presents some concepts which are not covered in detail until later chapters, in particular complex expressions and the `while` loop. These are described in order to show what it is possible to do, and to illustrate the "look and feel" of C. However, the student should not be expected to know these until they are covered in later chapters. The testbank for Chapter 1 covers only simple expressions, and does not cover the `while` statement or other control structures.

The two programming projects supplied for this chapter are intended primarily to get the student down to the computer center and learn how to use the system and to run a C program, so that they will be ready for the "real" programs in later chapters. The programs themselves are rather trivial. The first one is perhaps a little more difficult than the second, since it involves a floating point variable.

TRANSPARENCY MASTERS

Simple `printf` example
Variables and assignments
General form of a simple program
`printf` conversions
`scanf` conversions
Simple `scanf` example
Example: computing sums

ANSWERS TO EXERCISES

2. Here is the complete program:

```
#include <stdio.h>

main ()
{
    int     a, b, c, sum;

    printf("Input three integers:  ");
    scanf("%d %d %d", &a, &b, &c);

    sum = a + b + c;

    printf("%s%d%s\n",
        "Twice the sum of your integers plus 7 is ",
        2 * sum + 7, " -- bye!") ;

}
```

3. The following program prints a large letter C on the screen:

```
#include <stdio.h>

#define HEIGHT 17

main ()
{
    int     i = 0;

    printf("\n\nCCCCCCCCCCCCCC\n");
    while (i < HEIGHT)    {
        printf("CCC\n");
        i = i + 1;
    }
    printf("CCCCCCCCCCCCCC\n");
}
```

6. The following program computes the area of a rectangular lawn in square yards, square feet, square inches, given the length and width of the lawn in yards.

```
#include <stdio.h>

main ()
{
    int     Length, Width, SqYards, SqFeet,
        SqInches, SqMeters;

    /* conversion factor: sq in per sq yrd */
    int     cv_factor = 36 * 36;

     /* conversion factor: sq feet per sq yrd */
    int   cv_factor2 = 3 * 3;

    printf("%s\n%s%s",
        "Lawn area calculation",
        "Please enter length and width",
        " of your lawn in yards: ");
    scanf("%d %d", &Length, &Width);

    SqYards = Length * Width ;
    SqFeet = SqYards * cv_factor2 ;
    SqInches = SqYards * cv_factor ;

    printf("The area of your lawn is:\n");
    printf("    %d%s%d%s%d%s\n\n",
        SqYards, " sq. yards, ",
        SqFeet, " sq. feet, and ",
        SqInches, " sq. inches.");
}
```

7. The following program computes the value of some coins:

```c
#include <stdio.h>

main ()
{
    int     h,    /* number of half dollars */
        q,    /* number of quarters      */
        d,    /* number of dimes    */
        n,    /* number of nickels       */
        p,    /* number of pennies       */
        total;    /* total value of coins    */

    printf("The value of your change will be computed\n");
    printf("How many half dollars do you have?   ");
    scanf("%d", &h);
    printf("How many quarters do you have?   ");
    scanf("%d", &q);
    printf("How many dimes do you have?   ");
    scanf("%d", &d);
    printf("How many nickels do you have?   ");
    scanf("%d", &n);
    printf("How many pennies do you have?   ");
    scanf("%d", &p) ;

    printf("You entered: %4d half dollars,0, h);
    printf("%17d quarters0, q);
    printf("%17d dimes0, d);
    printf("%17d nickels0, n);
    printf("%17d pennies0, p);

    total = (h * 50) + (q * 25) + (d * 10)
            + (n * 5) + p ;
    printf("\n\n%s%d%s%d%s\n\n",
        "The value of your ", h + q + d + n + p,
        " coins is equivalent to ", total,
        " pennies.");
}
```

8. Here is the program from exercise 7 modified to print out the total in floating point format:

```
#include <stdio.h>

main ()
{
    int    h,       /* number of half dollars */
           q,       /* number of quarters     */
           d,       /* number of dimes   */
           n,       /* number of nickels      */
           p;       /* number of pennies      */

    float    total;    /* total value in dollars */

    printf("The value of your change is computed\n");
    printf("How many half dollars do you have?  ");
    scanf("%d", &h);
    printf("How many quarters do you have?  ");
    scanf("%d", &q);
    printf("How many dimes do you have?  ");
    scanf("%d", &d);
    printf("How many nickels do you have?  ");
    scanf("%d", &n);
    printf("How many pennies do you have?  ");
    scanf("%d", &p) ;

    printf("You entered: %4d half dollars,\n", h);
    printf("%17d quarters\n", q);
    printf("%17d dimes\n", d);
    printf("%17d nickels\n", n);
    printf("%17d pennies\n", p);

    total = (h * 0.50) + (q * 0.25) + (d * 0.10)
            + (n * 0.05) + (p * 0.01) ;
    printf("\n\n%s%d%s%.2f\n\n",
        "The value of your ", h + q + d + n + p,
        " coins is equivalent to $", total);
}
```

9. The integer printed by the program can be one of the following values:

-1	if an end-of-file is input (control-D on most unix systems),
0	if a non-numeric value is input before any valid numbers,
1	if one integer is entered followed by a non-numeric character,
2	if two integers are entered followed by a non-numeric character,
3	if three integers are entered.

12. The print statement which completes the program is the following:

```
printf("%d%s%d%s%d%s\n",
    input_value, " seconds is equivalent to ",
    minutes, " minutes and ",
    seconds, " seconds.")'
```

13. The following program converts seconds to hours, minutes, and seconds:

```
#include <stdio.h>

main ()
{
    int    input_value, hours, minutes, seconds;

    printf("Input the number of seconds:  ");
    scanf("%d", &input_value);

    /* First we convert from seconds to minutes and
        seconds, as in the previous exercise: */
    seconds = input_value % 60;
    minutes = input_value / 60;

    /* Then minutes are converted into
        hours and minutes: */
    hours = minutes / 60;
    minutes = minutes % 60;

    printf("%d%s%d%s%d%s%d%s\n",
        input_value, " seconds is equivalent to ",
        hours, " hours, ",
        minutes, " minutes, and ",
        seconds, " seconds.");
}
```

14. The program produces the following output:

```
sum = 1    i = 2
sum = 3    i = 3
sum = 6    i = 4
sum = 10    i = 5
sum = 15    i = 6
sum = 21    i = 7
sum = 28    i = 8
sum = 36    i = 9
sum = 45    i = 10
```

15. For the first variation, the following output is produced:

```
sum = 3     i = 2
sum = 7     i = 3
sum = 12    i = 4
sum = 18    i = 5
sum = 25    i = 6
sum = 33    i = 7
sum = 42    i = 8
sum = 52    i = 9
sum = 63    i = 10
```

For the second variation, the following output is produced:

```
sum = 1     i = 2
sum = 4     i = 3
sum = 10    i = 4
sum = 19    i = 5
sum = 31    i = 6
sum = 46    i = 7
sum = 64    i = 8
sum = 85    i = 9
sum = 109   i = 10
```

16. On our system, an end-of-file is signalled at the keyboard by a control-D. If either an inappropriate character or an end-of-file is entered before any numbers, the *find_sum* program produces the following output:

```
Count:    0
  Sum:    0.000000
```

17. *Find_sums* program modified to use type double instead of float:

```
#include <stdio.h>

main ()
{
    int   cnt = 0;
    double     sum = 0.0, x;

    printf("The sum of your numbers is computed.\n");
    printf("Input some numbers:   ");

    while (scanf("%lf", &x) == 1) {
        cnt = cnt + 1;
        sum = sum + x;
    }
    printf("\n%s%5d\n%s%12lf\n\n",
        "Count:", cnt,
        "  Sum:", sum);
}
```

18. With the first version, 4 gets printed. With the longer string, 43 is printed. The count includes special characters such as the tab (\t) and newline (\n).

20. With the terminal in its normal state, you won't see any output until the carriage return is pressed. The operating system sends keyboard input to the program line-by-line, and so the program does not begin to process the input until an entire line is entered. With *stty cbreak*, the operating system will deliver each character to the terminal as soon as it is entered. In this case you will see three characters for each one you type: one is the echo of your input, the other two are output by the program. With *stty -echo*, echoing is turned off, and you will only see two characters for each character entered.

PROGRAMMING PROJECT 1-1

Purpose: Practice using text editor and compiler, and `printf` and `scanf` statements.

For this assignment you will write a shoe store inventory program which inputs the user's shoe size and responds with the selection of available styles. Unfortunately this is one of those stores which never has anything in your size. Therefore the program simply runs as shown below (user input shown in boldface):

```
Welcome to ANSI's shoe emporium.
Please enter your shoe size: 8.5

Sorry, I don't have anything in size 8.5.
```

The last line of output should be exactly as shown above, with a single space before the number and a period following. (This forces you to use a field width specification for output.) Use a `float` variable for the shoe size.

Don't forget about READABILITY of your program:

> ● Put a COMMENT at the head of your program giving your name, the date, and the purpose of the program. Use comments elsewhere in the program where they will help make it more understandable.
>
> ● Use MNEMONIC VARIABLE NAMES -- "ShoeSize", for example, is much more descriptive than "X".
>
> ● Use WHITE SPACE freely to make the structure of the program apparent.

Also, don't forget to prompt the user for input.

PROGRAMMING PROJECT 1-2

Purpose: Practice using text editor and compiler, and `printf` and `scanf` statements.

Write a program which inputs a date in the form `mm/dd/yy` and outputs a sentence giving the date in the form

Day *dd* of month *mm* of the year 19*yy*.

For example, given the input

    10/15/91

the program should output

    Day 15 of month 10 of the year 1991.

Hint: In order to skip past the delimeters (the "/"'s), read them into a `char` type variable. Use `int` variables for the month, day, and year. Note that we can't do any error checking on the input at this point.

Don't forget about READABILITY of your program:

> • Put a COMMENT at the head of your program giving your name, the date, and the purpose of the program. Use comments elsewhere in the program where they will help make it more understandable.

> • Use MNEMONIC VARIABLE NAMES -- `DayNumber`, for example, is much more descriptive than `X`.

> • Use WHITE SPACE freely to make the structure of the program apparent.

Also, don't forget to prompt the user for input.

CHAPTER 2

LEXICAL ELEMENTS, OPERATORS, AND THE C SYSTEM

The previous chapter presented a general introduction to ANSI C programming. In this chapter the presentation becomes more rigorous, with a formal description of the lexical elements, which are the "lowest level" aspects of the language's syntax. Important points are:

- The concept of "tokens" helps the student visualize how the compiler interprets a program. Identifiers, numeric constants, and string constants should be well-understood.

- Good commenting style is important to emphasize early on.

- The concept of variables as "boxes" for data. Show students how to read code and keep track of what is going on by drawing a box for each variable and updating the box when the variable changes value.

- Increment and decrement operators are likely to be a new concept to the student (as opposed to the ordinary $+$, $-$, $*$, $/$). Examples of their operation should be presented. The same applies to the various assignment operators.

- Expressions are one of the most important topics in any programming course. Show how complex expressions are built up from (or analyzed in terms of) simpler expressions. Eventually the rules of precedence and associativity must beocome second nature to students, so use numerous class examples.

- Compiler errors are often a source of discouragement to the beginning programming student. Examples of error messages should be presented to "demystify" the compiler output. Point out that often a single syntax error will result in a raft of compiler messages, many of which won't immediately be meaningful. The student should also be reassured that even experienced programmers encounter compiler messages, and to expect them as part of the program development process.

Finally, it has almost become a cliche that "the way to teach programming is through examples." Even at this early stage, students should be presented with complete programs, so that they begin to gain an intuitive understanding of the programming process as a whole, at the same time that they are studying the individual components of a program in detail.

Transparency Masters

Characters and the compilation process
The *sum* program
Comments
Keywords
Identifiers
Integer constants
String constants
Precedence and Associativity of Operators
Sample Expressions
Assignment operators and examples
The *prn_rand* program
Commenting style
Example of compiler errors

ANSWERS TO EXERCISES

1. No, "main" is not a keyword. It is an identifier which is used as a function name. Even though it is required in every C program, it is not built into the C language and is actually defined by the programmer.

2. Here are some keywords introduced so far in the text, and their uses:

```
char, int, float, long, double
        data type names, used to declare a variable of the indicated type

while, for, do
        control structures used to begin loops (repetitive statements)

if, else
        control structure names used in conditional (branching) statements
```

3. Any of the following are tokens:

```
"abcdef"    a string constant is considered to be a token
int         a keyword is a token
56          a constant value is a token
XYZ         any identifier is a token
+           any operator or punctuation mark is a token
```

4.   `3id`   is not an identifier, because it begins with a digit;
     `1_i_am`   is not an identifier, because it begins with a digit;
     `__yes`   is an identifier (but it is best to avoid identifiers which
                      begin with underscores);
     `one_i_aren't`   is not an identifier, because it contains a single quote;
     `o_no_o_no`   is an identifier;
     `me_to-2`   is not an identifier, because it contains the character "-";
     `00_go`   is not an identifier, because it begins with a digit;
     `xYshouldI`   is an identifier;
     `star*it`   is not an identifier, because it contains the character "*";
     `int`   is not an identifier, because it is a keyword.

5. Here is one possible format for introductory comments:

```
/***********************************************************
 *
 * Program:     name & brief description of program
 * Author:      programmer's name
 * Date:        date program was written
 * Purpose:     ...
 * Revised:      date, author, and brief description of each modification
 *
 ***********************************************************/
```

6. The symbol + can be used:
   - as an addition operator in an expression: `x = x + 1 ;`
   - within the increment operator ++: `x++;`
   - within a character or string constant:
           `printf("The value of X + Y is %d.\n", X + Y);`

7. On our system, a nested comment produces a compiler warning message, but the program will still compile correctly.

8. The following program converts a weight input in pounds and ounces into both kilograms and grams.

```
/* define symbolic constants for conversion factors: */
#define        kg_per_g   .001
#define        ozs_per_lb      16
#define g_per_oz     28

main ()
{
    int           Pounds, Ounces ;
    float         Grams, Kilograms ;

    /* print out message and prompt for user input: */
    printf("English - metric conversion progam.\n");
    printf("Enter the weight in pounds and ounces.\n") ;
    printf("Pounds: ") ;
    scanf("%d", &Pounds) ;
    printf("Ounces: ") ;
    scanf("%d", &Ounces) ;

    /* now convert weight into number of ounces: */
    Ounces = Ounces + Pounds * ozs_per_lb ;
    /* then convert ounces into grams */
    Grams = Ounces * g_per_oz ;
    Kilograms = Grams * kg_per_g ;

    /* finally print out answer */
    printf("\nThat's %g grams, or %g kilograms.\n",
            Grams, Kilograms) ;
}
```

9.

```
/* Test program to determine how  a+++b
 * is interpreted by the compiler
 */
main ()
{
      int         a, b;

      printf("Each test is made with a = 1 and b = 12.\n");
      a = 1;
      b = 12;
      printf("a+++b = %d\n", a+++b);
      a = 1;
      b = 12;
      printf("a++ + b = %d\n", a++ + b);
      a = 1;
      b = 12;
      printf("a + ++b = %d\n", a + ++b);
}
```

On our system, the program produces the following output:

```
Each test is made with a = 1 and b = 12.
a+++b = 13
a++ + b = 13
a + ++b = 14
```

10. The value of "++i" is always one greater than the value of "i++". Therefore the "while" loop will execute one more time if "i++" is used in place if "++i", and the powers of 2 up to 11 instead of 10 will be printed.

11. The following is the output of the program:

```
2  1  1
2  2  2
5  3  3
5  2  2
```

12. The addition operator + has higher precedence than the assignment operator =. If the first set of parentheses is removed, y will receive the value 5 since the value of z will be added before the assignment to y, although x will receive the same value. If the second set of parentheses is removed, a compiler error message will occur, since only a variable, not an addition expression, can occur on the left side of an assignment.

13. Here are the expressions, equivalent expressions, and values:

Expression	Equivalent Expression	Value
7 + c * -- d / e	7 + ((c * (--d)) / e)	4
2 * a % - b + c + 1	(((2 * a) % (- b)) + c) + 1	7
39 / - ++ e - + 29 % c	(39 / (-(++e))) - ((+29) % c)	-7
a += b += c += 1 + 2	a += (b += (c += (1 + 2)))	7
7 - + ++ a % (3 + b)	7 - ((+ (++a)) % (3 + b))	

The last expression causes a run-time error, because the right-hand side of the `%` operator will be zero.

14. An equivalent statement is:

```
a += (b += (c += 7));
```

After the statement, we have c = 10, b = 12, and a = 13.

15. Here is a more readable version of the program:

```
/* Compute the average of three floating numbers */

main ()
{
   float    First, Second, Third, Average ;

   printf("Enter three floating-point numbers: ") ;
   scanf("%f%f%f", &First, &Second, &Third) ;
   Average = (First + Second + Third) / 3.0 ;
   printf("The average of the three numbers is %f.\n",
                           Average) ;
}
```

16. The following program will fail to compile if the symbolic constant RAND_MAX is not provided in the standard library; otherwise it will compile and will print out the value of RAND_MAX.

```
#include <stdio.h>
#include <stdlib.h>

main ()
{ printf("The constant RAND_MAX is %d.\n", RAND_MAX);
}
```

17. The following program tests the distribution of values produced by rand.

```
#include <stdio.h>
#include <stdlib.h>

#define    NUM_TRIALS       500

main ()
{
    int   i, plus_cnt = 0, minus_cnt = 0;
    int   median = RAND_MAX/2 ;

    for (i = 0; i < NUM_TRIALS; i++)
       {
      if ( rand() > median )
        plus_cnt ++ ;
      else
        minus_cnt ++ ;

        printf("%10d\n", plus_cnt - minus_cnt);
       }
}
```

18. To modify the *prn_rand* program so that all numbers are in the range [0, 100], the line

```
printf("%12d", rand());
```

is replaced by

```
printf("%12d", rand() % 101);
```

(Note that we must take the random number modulus 101, not 100, if we want to include the value 100.)

19. Here is the *prn_rand* program modified to use the `while` construct:

```
main ()
{
    int    i = 0, n;

    printf("\n%s\n%s",
        "Some randomly distributed integers are printed.",
        "How many do you want to see?  ");
    scanf("%d", &n);

    while (i++ < n)    {
        if (i % 6 == 1)
        printf("\n");
        printf("%12d", rand());
    }
    printf("\n");
}
```

In changing `i++` to `++i`, we must change the `<` to `<=`:

```
while (++i <= n)
```

The rest of the program will remain the same.

PROGRAMMING PROJECT 2-1

Purpose: Translating a problem specification into computer code;
                    `printf` and `scanf` statements;
                    arithmetic expressions.

For this assignment you are to write a program which computes the volume of a cylinder. It will read in the radius and height of the cylinder, compute the volume according to the formula:

$$V = \pi \cdot R^2 \cdot H$$

where V is the volume, R is the radius, and H is the height, and then write out the volume. A sample run of the program, with user input in boldface, is shown below:

```
Program to compute volume of a cylinder.
Please enter the radius: 3.5
Now enter the height: 10.1

The volume is 388.69.
```

The last line of output should be exactly as shown above, with a single space before the number, two digits following the decimal point, and a period after the number. (This forces you to use a field width specification for output.)

Don't forget about READABILITY of your program:

- Put a COMMENT at the head of your program giving your name, the date, and the purpose of the program. Use comments elsewhere in the program where they will help make it more understandable.

- Use MNEMONIC VARIABLE NAMES in place of the algebraic symbols in the formula -- "Radius", for example, is much more descriptive than "R".

- Use BLANK SPACE freely to make the structure of the program apparent. (However, don't overdo it. For example, excess blank lines can actually detract from readability; in particular, don't double space the entire program.)

- Use a #define for π (3.14159).

Also, don't forget to prompt the user for input.

PROGRAMMING PROJECT 2-2

Purpose: Translating a problem specification into computer code;
             `printf` and `scanf` statements;
             arithmetic expressions.

For this assignment you are to write a program which uses the Ideal Gas Law to calculate the pressure of an "ideal gas" contained in a cube of a given size at a given temperature. The Ideal Gas Law is given by the following formula:

$$P \times V = n \times R \times T$$

where

> P is the pressure in atmospheres;
> V is the volume in cubic centimeters;
> $n = 6.02 \times 10^{23}$ ("Avogadro's Number", the number of molecules in one mole);
> $R = 1.363 \times 10^{-22}$ (the "gas constant");
> T is the temperature in degrees Kelvin.

The volume of the cubic container is of course given by the formula

$$V = L^3$$

where V is in cubic centimeters and L is in centimeters. Since people prefer to think in terms of degrees Centigrade instead of degrees Kelvin, your program should use the following conversion formula:

degrees Kelvin = degrees Centingrade + 273.16

Your task is to program each of the above formulas as one or more assignment statements, request input from the user, and print out the pressure in atmospheres. A sample run is shown below, with user input in boldface:

```
Enter the side of the cube in centimeters:  10.5
Enter the temperature in degrees Centigrade: 25.0
The pressure is 21.13 atmospheres.
```

CHAPTER 3

FLOW OF CONTROL

The previous chapter introduced basic concepts; this chapter introduces the actual control structures which will allow students to start writing "real" programs. The main objects of this chapter can be summarized as follows:

● *Flow of control* -- Up until now the flow of control has been top-to-bottom within the **main** function. Now students can alter the flow of control to execute actions repeatedly or conditionally. I like to contrast the different control structures via the "flow diagrams" shown in some of the transparency masters (the ones which show templates for the various control statements).

● *Looping structures* -- Many students will have been exposed to loops in one form or another, but those who have never programmed before wll gain a better conceptual understanding by first introducing the concept of a "loop", then describing an algorithm which involves a loop, and finally presenting the loop's implementation in terms of **while, do,** or **for** statements.

● *Branching or conditional control structures* -- The above remarks also apply to the branching control structures, the **if** and **switch** statements.

● *Nesting of statements* -- After introducing the statements themselves, students learn that a statement which is "under control of" one of the control structures can itself be a complex statement. The analogy of "Chinese Boxes" which are literally "nested" one inside another can be useful. This is diagrammed in the transparency masters which show more complex code examples.

● *Program formatting and indentation* With the nesting of control structures it is important to start students off right away following good rules of program formatting, and especially indentation. In every class example, it should be pointed out how the control structure is visually apparent from the indentation. At the same time students must be reminded that the computer does not see the indentation.

By the end of this chapter, having learned the majority of the "tool kit" of control structures, it is good to emphasize the coding of short fragments such as a single loop or switch statement. However, it is best to stick to relatively short programs at this point, since students should not get into the habit of writing large programs without using functions, which are introduced in the next section.

This chapter also introduces the first "real" programming projects. The first requires only the **if** and **while** statements. The A simple desk calculator using the **switch** statement second is somewhat harder and makes use of all the control structures. From this point on, students should be encouraged to include in their programs checks for validity of input as far as is possible, and in an interactive environment, to repeat an input request when an error is detected.

TRANSPARENCY MASTERS

Relational, equality, and logical operators
Operators and precedence
Truth tables
`if` statement template and simple example
Nested `if` statement
`while` statement template and simple example
`for` statement template and simple example
Nested `for` statement
`do` statement template and simple example
`switch` statement template
A simple desk calculator using `switch`

ANSWERS TO EXERCISES

1. *Original expression:*   *Equivalent expression without negation:*

```
! (a > b)                    a <= b    (not a < b)
! (a + 1 == b + 1)           a + 1 != b + 1
! (a <= b && c <= d)         (a > b) || (c > d)
! (a < 1 || b < 2 && c < 3)  (a >= 1) && (b >= 2 || c >= 3)
```

2. *Original expression:*   *Equivalent expression:*   *Value:*

```
a > b && c < d          (a > b) && (c < d)            0
a < ! b || ! ! a        (a < (! b)) || (! (! a))      1
a + b < ! c + c         (a + b) < ((! c) + c)         0
a - x || b * x && b / a (a - x) || (b * x) && (b / a) 1
```

3. The following program computes taxes using a while loop:

```
#define    FEDERAL_TAX_RATE    0.23
#define    STATE_TAX_RATE      0.07

main ()
{
    long double   salary, federal_tax, state_tax,
                  total_salary = 0, tot_fed_tax = 0,
               tot_state_tax = 0;

    /* loop as long as valid numeric input */
    printf("Enter salary for each employee :\n") ;
    while (scanf("%lf", &salary) == 1) {

        /* compute taxes */
        federal_tax = salary * FEDERAL_TAX_RATE;
        state_tax = salary * STATE_TAX_RATE;
        printf("Salary = %.2f, Fed Tx = %.2f, St Tx = %.2f\n",
               salary, federal_tax, state_tax);

        /* update totals */
        total_salary += salary;
        tot_fed_tax += federal_tax;
        tot_state_tax += state_tax;
    }

    /* print out totals at end */
    printf("\nTot Salary = %.2f, ", total_salary);
    printf("Tot Fed Tx = %.2f, ", tot_fed_tax);
    printf("Tot St Tx = %.2f\n", tot_state_tax);
}
```

4. The output of the code is as follows:

```
0 0
1 0
1 1
1 0
```

5. The error in both fragments of code is that the assignment operator "=" is used instead of the equality operator "==". As written, the code will actually assign the value 7 to the variable k . Since the value of an assignment expression is the value assigned, which in this case is nonzero, the test will be considered "true". In the first example, this will result in an infinite loop, even though k is set to 0 at the end of each iteration. In the second example, the error causes the body of the if statement to be executed regardless of the original value of k.

6. Logically, the value "1" (for "true") should be printed, since in mathematics the equation

$$1e+33 + .001 > 1e+33 - .001$$

is true. But on most machines the value "0" will be printed, since there is not sufficient precision to discriminate between the two values.

7. The output of the code is the single line:

7

The only print statement which is executed is the last one. The else is associated with if (j == 2)..., *not* with if (i == 1) ..., even though the indentation (incorrectly) suggests otherwise.

8. The do keyword, although not required with a while, is a legal statement in itself in C. The compiler interprets the first line as a do statement within a while statement, and only complains when it fails to find a while at the end of what it thinks is the do statement.

9. If the values of i and j are not changed within the loop, then the only case in which ++i != 7 will never be false is if i starts out greater than or equal to 7. Similarly, the only case in which j++ != 9 will never be false is if "j" starts out greater than 9. However, the only case in which i * j < 0 will not be false is if either i or j is negative, which means that either ++i != 7 or j++ != 9 will eventually be false and the loop will terminate.

10. Here is the solution using for-loops:

```
main ()
{
    int    I, N, Sum = 0;

    printf("Enter an integer: ");
    scanf("%d", &N);

    if (N >= 0) {
        /* N is non-negative, sum from N to 2 * N */
     printf("Summing from %d to %d.\n", N, 2 * N);
        for (I = N ; I <= 2 * N ; I++)
            Sum += I;
    }
    else  {
        /* N is negative, sum from 2 * N to N */
     printf("Summing from %d to %d.\n", 2 * N, N);
        for (I = 2 * N ; I <= N ; I++)
            Sum += I;
    }
    printf("Sum = %d.\n", Sum);
}
```

Here is the solution using while-loops:

```
main ()
{
    int   I, N, Sum = 0;

    printf("Enter an integer: ");
    scanf("%d", &N);

    if (N >= 0) {
        /* N is non-negative, sum from N to 2 * N */
     printf("Summing from %d to %d.\n", N, 2 * N);
        I = N;
        while (I <= 2 * N)  {
            Sum += I;
            I++;
        }
    }
    else  {
        /* N is negative, sum from 2 * N to N */
     printf("Summing from %d to %d.\n", 2 * N, N);
        I = 2 * N;
        while (I <= N)  {
            Sum += I;
            I++;
        }
    }
    printf("The sum is %d.\n", Sum);
}
```

11. The following code accomplishes the desired infinite loop:

```
for (;;)
    printf("   True forever!   ");
```

12. The code `while (-33.777) ...` is also an infinite loop. Any non-zero value, either integer or floating, is considered "true" in a conditional or looping statement.

13.

$e1 - e2$	Values of: $e1 != e2$	$e1 == e2$	$!(e1 == e2)$
zero	false	true	false
nonzero	true	false	true

14. Replace the `printf` by the following:

```
if (n == 1)
    printf("Enter a real number:\n");
else
    printf("Enter %d real numbers:\n", n);
```

15. The following program finds the maximum odd integer from n integers.

```
main ()
{
    int    cnt = 0, n, max, x;

    printf("The maximum of all odd integers is computed.\n");
    printf("Even integers will be ignored.\n");
    printf("How many integers do you wish to enter?  ");
    scanf("%d", &n);
    while (n <= 0)   {
        printf("\nERROR: Positive integer is required.\n");
        printf("How many integers do you wish to enter? ");
        scanf("%d", &n);
    }
    printf("\nEnter %d integers:  ", n) ;
    scanf("%d", &x);
    max = x;
    while (++cnt < n)   {
        scanf("%d", &x);
        if (x % 2 == 1)      /* Test for odd integer */
            if (max < x)
                max = x;
    }
    printf("\nMaximum odd value:  %d\n", max);
}
```

16. On some systems, the "for" loop will not terminate because the value of x will never exactly equal "9.9", due to round-off error in floating addition. In this case we can guarantee that the loop will always terminate by replacing the "not equal" test with a "less than" test:

```
double    sum = 0.0, x;

printf("%5s%15s\n", "Value", "Running sum");
printf("%5s%15s\n", "-----", "-----------");
for (x = 0.0; x < 9.9; x += 0.1)  {
    sum += x;
    printf("%5.1f%15.1f\n", x, sum);
}
```

17. As written the code will be an infinite loop, since the termination condition, ++i, will always be non-zero or "true" given that i starts out at 1.

18. The following program computes the sum of all integers between two given numbers divisible by a given number .

```
main ()
{
    int k, m, n, i, sum = 0;

    printf("The sum of integers between m and n ");
    printf("divisible by k:\n");
    printf("Enter value for k:   ");
    scanf("%d", &k);
    while (k < 1)  {
        printf("\nERROR  k must be greater than 1.\n");
        printf("Enter value for k:   ");
        scanf("%d", &k);
    }

    printf("Enter lower bound (m):   ");
    scanf("%d", &m);
    printf("Enter upper bound (n):   ");
    scanf("%d", &n);

    for (i = m ; i <= n ; i++)
        if (i % k == 0)    /* test for m divisible by k */
            sum += i;

    printf("The sum of integers between %d and %d", m, n);
    printf(" divisble by %d is %d.\n", k, sum);
}
```

19. The value of x = 0 is 0 or "false" and so the right side of the && is not executed. Similarly, the value of x = 777 is 777 or "true" and so the right side of the || is not executed. The values of a and b are never modified. The output of the code is:

```
0  0  0
0  0  777
```

20.

Original Expression	Equivalent Expression	Value
a && b && c	(a && b) && c	1
a && b || c	(a && b) || c	1
a || b && c	a || (b && c)	1
a || !b && !!c + 4	a || ((!b) && ((!(!c)) + 4))	1

22. The following program produces the truth table for the first boolean expression. (The #define can be modified to produce the truth table for a different boolean expression.)

```
/* Print a truth table for an arbitray boolean function
 * of 4 boolean vars.  The #define below specifies the
 * boolean expression, in terms of the four boolean
 * variables b1, b2, b3, b4
 */

#define BOOLEX (b1 || b2 || b3 || b4)

main ()
{
    int b1, b2, b3, b4, cnt = 0;

    printf("\n%5s%5s%5s%5s%5s%7s\n\n",
            "cnt", "b1", "b2", "b3", "b4", "expr");
    for (b1 = 0 ; b1 <= 1 ; ++b1)
       for (b2 = 0 ; b2 <= 1 ; ++b2)
          for (b3 = 0 ; b3 <= 1 ; ++b3)
             for (b4 = 0 ; b4 <= 1 ; ++b4)
                printf("%5d%5d%5d%5d%5d%7d0,
                        ++cnt, b1, b2, b3, b4, BOOLEX);
    putchar('\n');
}
```

Here is the truth table generated for the first boolean expression:

cnt	b1	b2	b3	b4	expr
1	0	0	0	0	0
2	0	0	0	1	1
3	0	0	1	0	1
4	0	0	1	1	1
5	0	1	0	0	1
6	0	1	0	1	1
7	0	1	1	0	1
8	0	1	1	1	1
9	1	0	0	0	0
10	1	0	0	1	1
11	1	0	1	0	1
12	1	0	1	1	1
13	1	1	0	0	1
14	1	1	0	1	1
15	1	1	1	0	1
16	1	1	1	1	1

Here is the truth table generated for the second boolean expression:

cnt	b1	b2	b3	b4	expr
1	0	0	0	0	0
2	0	0	0	1	0
3	0	0	1	0	0
4	0	0	1	1	0
5	0	1	0	0	0
6	0	1	0	1	0
7	0	1	1	0	0
8	0	1	1	1	0
9	1	0	0	0	1
10	1	0	0	1	1
11	1	0	1	0	0
12	1	0	1	1	1
13	1	1	0	0	0
14	1	1	0	1	0
15	1	1	1	0	0
16	1	1	1	1	0

23. The code generates an infinite loop starting with '1' and repeating the sequence "234". The '5' is never printed.

```
1234234234234234234234234......
```

24. The mathematical operation "min(x, y, z)" can be coded as

```
(x < y) ? ( (x < z) ? x : z) : ( (y < z) ? y : z)
```

The operation min(x, y, z, w) can be coded as:

```
(x < y) ? ( (x < z) ? ( ( (x < w) ? x : w )
                        : ( (z < w) ? z : w ) ) )
        : ( (y < z) ? ( ( (y < w) ? y : w )
                        : ( (z < w) ? z : w ) ) )
```

PROGRAMMING PROJECT 3-1

Purpose: logical expressions;
               `if` and `while` statements;
               input error checking

This assignment is to write a program to play the well-known game of Nim. The game starts with some number of stones in a pile. The players take turns removing either one or two stones at each move. The player who takes the last stone loses. It is easy to program an optimal strategy for Nim: Take the remainder on dividing the number of stones left by three; this will be 0, 1, or 2. If it is 0, then take 2 stones; if it is 2, take 1 stone. If the remainder is 1, then the game cannot be won, assuming the opponent is also playing the optimal strategy; however, the program still puts up a good show of it, and takes one stone (delaying the inevitable and giving the opponent more chances to make a mistake).

Your program should start out by asking the user for the number of stones to start with, and then asking who moves first (0 = program, 1 = user). It then runs in a loop, alternating turns between the program and the user. The program chooses one or two stones according to the above strategy, and asks the user how many stones s/he wishes to take. When the number of stones reaches zero, the program announces the winner.

An important part of this assignment is input error checking. Your program should check for the following errors:

      initial number of stones must be greater than zero;
      "who moves first" must be 0 or 1;
      number of stones removed by user at each move must be one or two,
      and not more than the number remaining.

If an error is detected, the program should output an appropriate error message and repeat the input request. For this exercise, it is not necessary to check for non-numeric input.

PROGRAMMING PROJECT 3-2

Purpose: Using all control structures.

A presidential candidate recently pledged 1) to greatly simplify the tax laws, and 2) to rewrite all the government's software in C. This sent his staff scrambling, since they did not know C (nor how to write simple laws). They finally came up with the following rules:

1) Taxable income is equal to gross income minus the standard deduction minus $1,000 for each exemption. The standard deduction is $3,000. The maximum number of allowable exemptions is 12. A bright student intern remembered to add the rule that the taxable income could not be less than zero.

2) The tax rate is computed from the following table based on the filing status and the taxable income:

Filing status	Taxable income	Tax rate
Single	less than $5,000	15%
	$5,000 - $20,000	22%
	more than $20,000	31%
Married	less than $10,000	15%
	$10,000 - $40,000	22%
	more than $40,000	31%
Married filing jointly	less than $7,000	17%
	$7,000 - $25,000	24%
	more than $25,000	33%

3) The total tax due is the taxable income times the tax rate. The student intern pointed out that this is not a "marginal tax rate", but just a simple percentage calculation. The rest of the staff decided that since the student intern was so smart, she should be given the job of writing a demonstration program for this in C, and they all left for the campaign trail.

The program is to run in a loop. Each time it asks for the following:

> Taxpayer ID (social security #) -- any integer
> Filing Status -- single character, must be 'S' for single, 'M' for married, 'J' for married filing jointly
> Gross Income -- any floating number (negative allowed, representing a loss)
> Number of Exemptions -- an integer between 0 and 12, inclusive.

It computes and prints out the taxable income, tax rate, and tax amount, and repeats for the next taxpayer. Any non-numeric input for the taxpayer ID will terminate the loop, and the program then prints a summary including the number of taxpayers processed, the average tax amount, the highest tax amount, and the taxpayer ID of the highest tax amount.

CHAPTER 4

FUNCTIONS AND STRUCTURED PROGRAMMING

Now that students have learned the basic "tool-kit" of control structures for programming, they learn to break up their code into logical pieces. It has been my experience that students are often resistant to the idea of organizing their programs into functions, believing that it decreases efficiency and constrains their style. To the extent that this is true it is probably because their algorithmic design is not as well structured as it could be. Students must be encouraged to avoid plunging directly into writing code when given a programming task, and instead go through the process of functional decomposition and pseudo code, as described in the text. Important points here are:

- The basic mechanism of function call and return. I like to emphasize that a function can be called from several different places, and that it always returns to the place it was called from.

- Parameter passing and returned function values as a means of communication between the function and its caller. The concept of parameters seems to be much more difficult for students to grasp than the basic idea of functions. Only devote a small amount of class time to functions without parameters, then move directly into examples of functions with parameters. Note that in this textbook global variables have not yet been introduced.

- Emphasize the one-to-one matching of formal parameters and actual parameters: there must be the same number of actual as formal parameters, and the types should match (do not rely on the compiler's automatic type conversion). Also, point out that the parameter matching is based on position, not on name.

- Top-down algorithmic design, and how it translates directly into function definition. I like to present at least one detailed and realistic design example, going from the statement of the problem, through its decomposition into subproblems, implementing each subproblem as a function, and finally showing a working program.

If students are exposed to many examples of complex problems elegantly implemented in short, easy to understand functions, they will gain a better appreciation of structured programming. I like to describe functions as "black boxes" with their own enviroment, and show how the boxes are strung together to make a complete program. The parameters and returned function values are the connecting links between the boxes.

The issue of scope is not of great significance at this point. Unlike other languages, C does not allow nested function definitions, and nested blocks with variable declarations are not introduced until a later chapter. But do point out that an "X" in one function is entirely different from an "X" in another function.

TRANSPARENCY MASTERS

Function definition and example
`return` statement and example
Function prototype and example
Top Down Design Example: `read_and_prn_data`
Top Down Design Example: The Game of Heads or Tails
Call-by-Value

ANSWERS TO EXERCISES

1. The only change is to add an infinite loop in the "prn_message" function.

```
void prn_message (void)
{
    printf("Message for you:   ");
    printf("Have a nice day!\n");
    for  (;;)
        printf("%34s\n", "Have a nice day!");
}

main ()
{
    prn_message();
}
```

2. The following function definitions compute integer squares and cubes:

```
int Square (int N)
{
    return (N * N);
}

int Cube (int N)
{
    return (N * N * N);
}
```

3. The following program uses the above functions to print a table of squares and cubes:

```
main ()
{
    int     I;

    printf("\n\n%12s %12s %12s\n", "N:", "N**2", "N**3");

    for (I = 1 ; I <= 25 ; I++)
        printf("%12d %12d %12d\n", I, Square(I), Cube(I));
}
```

4. The program can be fixed by adding an if-statement to the prn_random_numbers function:

```
void prn_random_numbers (int k)
{
    int     i, r, smallest, biggest;
    int     min(int, int), max(int, int), rand(void);

    if (k > 0)   {
        r = smallest = biggest = rand();
        printf("\n%12d", r);
        for (i = 1 ; i < k ; ++i)   {
            if (i % 5 == 0)
                printf("\n");
            r = rand();
            smallest = min(r, smallest);
            biggest = max(r, biggest);
            printf("%12d", r);
        }
        printf("\n\n%d random numbers printed.\n", k);
        printf("Minimum: %7d\nMaximum: %7d\n\n",
                    smallest, biggest);
    }
    else
        printf("\n\nNo random numbers printed.\n\n");
}
```

5. With the for-loop modified as indicated, the same number of random numbers will be printed, but the format will be different because the value of "i" in the "i % 5" test will be different for a given number. The following change restores the correct format:

```c
void prn_random_numbers (int k)
{
    int     i, r, smallest, biggest;
    int     min(int, int), max(int, int), rand(void);

    if (k > 0)    {
        r = smallest = biggest = rand();
        printf("\n%12d", r);
        for (i = 2 ; i <= k ; ++i)    {
            if (i % 5 == 1)
                printf("\n");
            r = rand();
            smallest = min(r, smallest);
            biggest = max(r, biggest);
            printf("%12d", r);
        }
        printf("\n%d random numbers printed.\n", k);
        printf("Minimum: %7d\nMaximum: %7d\n\n",
                smallest, biggest);
    }
    else
        printf("\n\nNo random numbers printed.\n\n");
}
```

6. The `main` function of the program is modified to accept a seed value from the user. The `prn_random_numbers` function remains the same.

```c
main ()
{
    int     n, seed;
    void    prn_random_numbers(int);

    printf("Some random numbers are to be printed.\n");
    printf("How many would you like to see?  ");
    scanf("%d", &n);

    printf("Enter a starting seed value:  ");
    scanf("%d", &seed);
    srand(seed);

    prn_random_numbers(n);
}
```

8. The following program computes the minimum of two numbers of type double.

```
double dmin (double x, double y) {
   if (x < y)
      return(x);
   else
      return(y);  }

main () {
   double j, k, m;

   printf("Input two floating point numbers:  ");
   scanf("%lf%lf", &j, &k);
   m = dmin(j, k);
   printf("\n%lf is the minimum of %lf and %lf\n\n",
m, j, k);  }
```

The following program computes the minimum of 4 doubles. A clever way to get the minimum of 4 values is to call the dmin of 2 values three times:

```
double dmin (double x, double y)
{
   if (x < y)
      return(x);
   else
      return(y);
}

double dmin4 (double x, double y, double z, double w)
{
   return(dmin(dmin(x, y), dmin(z, w)));
}

main ()
{
   double a, b, c, d, m;

   printf("Input four floating point numbers:  ");
   scanf("%lf%lf%lf%lf", &a, &b, &c, &d);
   m = dmin4(a, b, c, d);
   printf("%lf is the minimum of %lf, %lf, %lf, and %lf\n",
           m, a, b, c, d);
}
```

9. The following program prints hailstone sequences.

```
void hailstones (int n)
{
    int     i;

    printf("\n\nHailstones generated by %d:\n\n", n);
    printf("%d   ", n);

    for (i = 1 ; n != 1 ; i++)  {
        if (n % 2 == 0)
            n = n / 2;         /*n is even*/
        else
            n = 3 * n + 1;   /*n is odd*/

        if (i % 6 == 0)
            putchar('\n');
        printf("%d   ", n);
    }
    printf("Number of hailstones generated:  %d\n", i);
}

main ()
{
    int     n;

    printf("Program to print hailstone sequences.\n");
    printf("Enter starting integer:   ");
    scanf("%d", &n);
    hailstones(n);
}
```

10.

```
/* Program to test Goldbach's conjecture
 * that every even integer > 2 can be expressed
 * as the sum of two integers.
 */
#include <stdio.h>
#include <math.h>

/* The lower and upper limits of our test: */
#define         START           700
#define         FINISH          1100

/* Determine if a number is prime
 * NOTE: Many sophisticated prime-testing algorithms
 * exist.  This uses a simple "brute-force" approach
 * of dividing the number by every odd number to see
 * if it is divisible.  We stop at the * square root
 * of the number to avoid redundant checks.
 * ASSUMES that the number is > 2
 */
int is_prime (int n)
{
        int  i, stop = (int) sqrt ((double) n);

        for (i = 3 ; i <= stop ; i += 2)
                if (n % i == 0)
                        /* found a divisor, not prime */
                        return 0;

        /* it's prime if we fall thru above loop */
        return 1;
}
```

```c
/* Check Goldbach's conjecture for a single even number
 * This also uses a "brute-force" approach.
 * For each odd integer starting at 3, we see if the
 * integer is prime and if the number minus the prime
 * is also prime.  If it is, we have expressed the
 * number as the sum of two primes.
 * we stop the test at the number divided by 2
 * (But a stopping condition should not be necessary
 *  if the conjecture is true!)
 * Note not necessary to try 2 since 2 plus any other
 * prime is odd, and the conjecture applies to even #s
 */
int sum_2_primes (int n)
{
        int  p1, stop = n / 2;

        for (p1 = 3 ; p1 <= stop ; p1 += 2)
              if (is_prime(p1))
                  if (is_prime(n - p1)) {
                      printf("%6d = %5d + %5d0,
                            n, p1, n - p1);
                      return;
                  }
        printf("Goldbach's conjecture failed for %d!\n", n);
}

main ()
{
        int  n;

        printf("Testing Goldbach's conjecture ");
        printf("from %d to %d.\n", START, FINISH);
        for (n = START ; n <= FINISH ; n += 2)
            sum_2_primes(n);
}
```

11. If the format %10s is changed to %15s, the word "heads" or "tails" will be preceded by 10 blanks instead of 5 blanks. This means that the lines of output will contain 105 characters instead of 70 characters, and will therefore wrap-around on most terminals which have only 80 characters in a line. The problem can be fixed by changing the if (i % 7 == 0) ... to if (i % 5 == 0) ...

If the call the srand is moved so that it is the first statement in the body of the for-loop, then the random number generator will be initialized to the same value each time around the loop, and will therefore give the same number each time. The output will be either all "heads" or all "tails".

12. In the following function, the "if-else" statement is replaced with a conditional operator:

```
void report_a_win (int coin)
{
    printf("I have %s, you win.\n",
           (coin == 0) ? "heads" : "tails");
}
```

13. If a letter instead of a number is input to the *run_sums* program, the scanf inside the while-loop will return a value of 0, since it did not find data in the %d format. Therefore the program will exit the loop and will terminate, just as if an end-of-file signal were entered.

PROGRAMMING PROJECT 4

Purpose: Top-down design using functions.

Write a program to print a calendar for any month of any year from 1900 on. Here is a sample run, with user input in boldface:

```
Enter month number: 13
Month must be between 1 and 12, please re-enter: 11
Enter year: 90
Year must be 1900 or later, please re-enter: 1990

November, 1990
   S    M    T    W    T    F    S
                            1    2    3
   4    5    6    7    8    9   10
  11   12   13   14   15   16   17
  18   19   20   21   22   23   24
  25   26   26   27   28   29   30
```

This appears to be a simple problem but it is rich in subproblems and functionalization. It turns out that most of the program involves finding the day of the week on which the month starts. You do this my knowing that January 1, 1900 fell on a Monday, and then finding the number of days difference between that day and the first day of the month for the calendar. This difference mod 7 tells you the day of the week. Finding the number of days from 1/1/1900 to the first day of any other month can be further broken down into the following subproblems:

1. Number of days in whole years (i.e. (Year - 1900 - 1) * 365);
2. One for each year in the above range which is a leap year;
3. The number of days in each month from January to Month - 1.

Remember the rule for leap years: A year is a leap year if it is divisible by 4, *unless* it is divisible by 100, in which case it's not a leap year, *UNLESS* it's also divisible by 400, in which case it is a leap year.

Use the method of top-down design, breaking the problem into subproblems and each subproblem into further subproblems, until it is easy to code each subproblem as a C function. At this point, your problem decomposition should show the basic structure of the program, as well as making the code modular and easy to read and debug. Typical functions you might find useful:

Given a year, return 1 if it is a leap year and 0 otherwise;

Given a month number and a year, return the number of days in that month, using a switch statement. (It needs the year so February will have 29 days in a leap year.)

Given a month number, print the name of the month.

CHAPTER 5

CHARACTER PROCESSING

Character processing is not quite text processing (strings won't be introduced until much later), but even so this will be new for students who have only been exposed to computers as number-crunchers. By the same token, simple programs that manipulate text tend to be more interesting than programs that process numbers. Some important objectives are the following:

- Characters are data to the computer just as numbers are, and in fact are represented as small integers. A simple demonstration program which prints out the integers from 32 to 126 with their corresponding characters is useful.

- The use of `getchar` and `putchar` is an alternative to `scanf` and `printf`. It should be noted that they operate at a slightly "lower level", without conversions or skipping of white space.

- Many students are confused by the effect of the operating system's I/O buffer. They don't understand why a `getchar()` doesn't return a character to the program as soon as it is typed. I find it necessary to explain how the O.S. buffers input and does not deliver it to the program until a newline is pressed. I also explain "raw mode" input as an alternative, and why it usually isn't used (so that backspace, etc. can be used to correct typing errors).

- Go over the macros in *ctype.h*, Although students should not necessarily have each one memorized, they should know the most common ones and be aware of the existence of the others. The testbank covers only the most commonly used macros: `isalpha`, `isupper`, `islower`, `isspace`, `ispunct`, `toupper`, and `tolower`.

Since there is not a lot of conceptually new or difficult material in chapter 5, many of the test bank questions involve using functions to perform simple tasks. This provides additional practice with functions, and gets the student into the habit of "packaging" programming tasks into functions.

46

TRANSPARENCY MASTERS

Some Character Constants and ther corresponding integer values
Non-printing or control characters
Printing characters and their numeric values
caps example -- capitalize lower case letters and double space
The macros in *ctype.h*
caps example -- a portable version
A more complex example -- counting words
A couple of common programming errors

ANSWERS TO EXERCISES

1.

```
/*    Program to read characters from the keyboard,
 *       write each letter 3 times followed by newline
 *       ignore newlines in input
 *       echo other chars
 */

#include <stdio.h>
#include <ctype.h>

main ()
{
    int    Ch;

    while ( (Ch = getchar()) != EOF)
        if (isalpha(Ch))   {
            /* it's a letter, output 3 times */
            putchar(Ch);
            putchar(Ch);
            putchar(Ch);
            putchar('\n');
        }
        else
            if (Ch != '\n')
                putchar(Ch);
}
```

2.

```c
/* Program to read chars until a '#'
 * Counts occurrences of 'a', 'b', 'c'
 */

#include <stdio.h>
#include <ctype.h>

main ()
{
    int Ch, aCount = 0, bCount = 0, cCount = 0;

    while  ( (Ch = getchar()) != '#')
       if (Ch == 'a')
          aCount++;
       else if (Ch == 'b')
          bCount++;
       else if (Ch == 'c')
          cCount++;

     printf("'a' occurred %d times, ", aCount);
     printf("'b' %d times, and 'c' %d times.\n",
           bCount, cCount);
}
```

3.

```c
/* Program to read chars until end-of-file
 * Counts occurrences of 'a', 'b', 'c'
 */

#include <stdio.h>
#include <ctype.h>

main ()
{
    int Ch, aCount = 0, bCount = 0, cCount = 0;

    while  ( (Ch = getchar()) != EOF)
       if (Ch == 'a')
          aCount++;
       else if (Ch == 'b')
          bCount++;
       else if (Ch == 'c')
          cCount++;

     printf("'a' occurred %d times, ", aCount);
     printf("'b' %d times, and 'c' %d times.\n",
           bCount, cCount);
}
```

4.

```
/* Read and write characters,
 * Write all vowels in uppercase,
 *  all non-vowels in lowercase
 */

#include <stdio.h>
#include <ctype.h>

/* Test to see if a character is a vowel */
int isvowel (char Ch)
{
    switch (Ch) {
        case 'a': case 'e': case 'i': case 'o': case 'u':
        case 'A': case 'E': case 'I': case 'O': case 'U':
            return(1);
        default:
            return(0);
    }
}

main ()
{
    int    Ch;

    while ( (Ch = getchar()) != EOF) {
        if (isvowel(Ch))  {
            /* it's a vowel, change to uppercase
             * if not already
             */
            if (islower(Ch))
                Ch = toupper(Ch);
        }
        else
            /* not a vowel, change to lowercase
             * if a letter and uppercase
             */
            if (isalpha(Ch) && isupper(Ch))
                Ch = tolower(Ch);
        putchar(Ch);
    }
}
```

5. The program below exercises the `isprint` macro. On our system, it produced the following output:

```
Backspace is not considered printable.
Newline is not considered printable.
Space is considered printable.
Tab is not considered printable.
```

```c
/* Program to determine which space characters are
 * considered printable
 */
#include <stdio.h>
#include <ctype.h>

main ()
{
    printf("Backspace is ");
    if (! isprint('\b'))
     printf("not ");
    printf("considered printable.\n");

    printf("Newline is ");
    if (! isprint('\n'))
     printf("not ");
    printf("considered printable.\n");

    printf("Space is ");
    if (! isprint(' '))
     printf("not ");
    printf("considered printable.\n");

    printf("Tab is ");
    if (! isprint('\t'))
     printf("not ");
    printf("considered printable.\n");
}
```

6.

```c
/*   Program to reformat a text file
 *   Each line will contain approximately N characters
 */

#include <stdio.h>
#include <ctype.h>

#define         N       30

main ()
{
    int     Ch, LineSize = 0;

    /* loop until end of file */
    while ( (Ch = getchar()) != EOF)   {
        if (LineSize < N)   {
            /* left of column N, change newline to blank
             & count the char */
            if (Ch == '\n')
                Ch = ' ';
            LineSize++;
        }
        else
            /* right of column N, start new line
             on space or newline, zero count */
            if (isspace(Ch))   {
                Ch = '\n';
                LineSize = 0;
            }
            else
                /* right of column N but not a space,
                just count the char */
                LineSize++;

        putchar(Ch);
    }

    /* at end of file, output a newline
           if there is a partial line written */
    if (LineSize > 0)
        putchar('\n');
}
```

7.
```
/* Program to indent all lines in a text file by N blanks
 */

#include <stdio.h>
#include <ctype.h>

#define    N     4

main ()
{
    int Ch, i;

    /* loop for all lines in file, until EOF */
    while ( (Ch = getchar()) != EOF)     {

        /* first write out N blanks in a for-loop */
        for (i = 0 ; i < N ; i++)
            putchar(' ');

        /* loop for all characters in line, until newline */
        /* we assume the unix convention that  */
        /*  a newline always precedes EOF      */
        /* note first character already in Ch  */
        while  (Ch != '\n')  {
            putchar(Ch);
            Ch = getchar();
        }
        putchar('\n');
    }
}
```

8.
```
/* Program to print a diamond of height & width N */

#include <stdio.h>
#include <ctype.h>

#define    N    33

/* subroutine to write a character N times */
void repeat (char C, int Count)
{
    while (Count-- > 0)
        putchar(C);
}

main ()
{
    char    C = 'X';
    int i;

    /* first draw upper half of diamond */
    for (i = 1 ; i <= N ; i++)  {

        /* first write N-i blanks to move cursor */
        repeat(' ', N - i);

        /* then write i*2 characters for body of diamond */
        repeat(C, i * 2);
        putchar('\n');
    }

    /* now do the lower half */
    for (i = 1 ; i <= N ; i++)  {
        repeat(' ', i);
        repeat(C, (N - i) * 2);
        putchar('\n');
    }
}
```

9. The for-loop produces the following output (in an infinite loop):

```
0132132132132132...
```

The `printf` statement prints the letters A, B, and C in two different ways: once as a side-effect of the `putchar`, the other as the returned value from `putchar` into the `printf` call. The exact output may vary from system to system, but one possibility is:

```
CBAABC
```

10. Without the parentheses in the `while` condition, the `!=` will have higher precedence than the assignment, and so it is the same as:

```
while (c = (getchar() != EOF))
    putchar(c);
```

The variable `c` will be assigned the result of the comparison, 1 if not end of file, and 0 at end of file. The loop will write one character for each character in the file, but the characters it writes will all be character code 1 (which happens to be control-A, a non-printing character, in ASCII).

11. Because of the modular design of the heads-or-tails program, the only function which must be changed to input *h* or *t* instead of '0' or '1' is `get_call_from_user`. It turns out that putting a space before the `%c` causes `scanf` to skip any white space before inputting a character. Note that either lowercase or uppercase is accepted.

```
/*return 0 for heads and 1 for tails */
int get_call_from_user (void)
{
    char    Ch;

    scanf(" %c", &Ch);
    while (Ch != 'h' && Ch != 't' &&
            Ch != 'H' && Ch != 'T')   {
        printf("ERROR: 'h' for heads, 't' for tails\n");
        scanf(" %c", &Ch);
    }
    return  Ch == 't' || Ch == 'T';
}
```

12. The following program to reads and writes a text file with all vowels removed.

```
#include <stdio.h>
#include <ctype.h>

/* Test to see if a character is a vowel */
int isvowel (char Ch)
{
    switch (Ch) {
        case 'a':  case 'e':  case 'i':  case 'o':  case 'u':
        case 'A':  case 'E':  case 'I':  case 'O':  case 'U':
            return(1);
        default:
            return(0);
    }
}
```

```
main ()
{
    int     Ch;
    /* loop for each character, until end of file */
    while ( (Ch = getchar()) != EOF)

        /* check for a vowel */
        if (! isvowel(Ch))

            /* write the character if not */
            putchar(Ch);
}
```

13.

```
/* text file crunching program
 * reduces any sequence of space characters to a
 * single space character in order to preserve
 * some of the original file's structure, a
 * sequence of space characters containing a newline
 * is reduced to a newline, otherwise to a space
 */
#include <stdio.h>
#include <ctype.h>

/* this function is called after the first space
 * character is read. It keeps reading until a
 * non-space character is read, then outputs either
 * a blank or a newline. It is passed the first char
 * so it knows whether to output a blank or newline
 * at the end it returns the non-blank char so caller
 * can check for EOF
 */
int skip_blanks (int ch)
{
    char outchar = ' ';

    do  {
        if (ch == '\n')
            outchar = '\n';
        ch = getchar();
    }  while (isspace(ch));
    putchar(outchar);
    return ch;
}

main ()
{
    int  ch;

    do {
        ch = getchar();
        if (isspace(ch))
            ch = skip_blanks(ch);
        if (ch != EOF)
            putchar(ch);
    } while (ch != EOF);
}
```

14.

```
/* Simple "pretty printing" program for C programs
 * Sophisticated pretty printers recognize the
 * program's keywords.  Since strings haven't been
 * introduced yet, this uses the simple rule:
 *    Increases indentation by 4 characters when a {
 *        is encountered.
 *    Inserts a newline after each {, unless already
 *        followed by newline,
 *    Decreases indentation by 4 characters when a }
 *        is encountered.
 *    Adds a newline just before each }, unless a
 *        newline is already there.
 *    Also adds an extra newline after } brings us
 *        back to top level, to space between function
 *        definitions.
 * NOTE: This program does not check for comments,
 *    string constants, or character constants,
 *    and therefore won't work right for programs
 *    that contain } or { characters within these
 *    consructs (such as this program).
 */
#include <stdio.h>
#include <ctype.h>

#define       INDENT_STEP    4;

main ()
{
    int  ch, i, indent = 0;
    int  newline_pending = 0;

    while ((ch = getchar()) != EOF) {
        if (ch == '0)
        /* we delay newlines until a non-blank char
         * is read so indentation can be reduced on
         * a } and extra newlines after { eliminated
         */
            newline_pending = 1;
        else {
            if (ch == '}')
                indent -= INDENT_STEP;
            if (newline_pending) {
                newline_pending = 0;
                putchar('0);
                for (i = 0 ; i < indent ; ++i)
                    putchar(' ');
            }
```

(14. continued)

```
                    putchar(ch);
                    if (ch == '{') {
                        indent += INDENT_STEP;
                        newline_pending = 1;
                    }
                    if (ch == '}' && indent == 0)
                        putchar('0);
                }
            }
        }
```

15. The first blank following the AAAAA comes from the putchar just before the for-loop. The second blank comes from the first iteration of the for-loop with i = 0, which causes the character 'A' + 0 (= 'A') to be printed zero times, but the putchar within the for-loop is still executed.

PROGRAMMING PROJECT 5-1

Purpose: Character processing, more practice with functions.

Write a C program which reads a sequence of words, one per line with no blanks, and finds which words satisfy either of two conditions:

> • contain three (or more) consecutive characters in strict alphabetic order (e.g. caLMNess), or

> • all of whose letters are in alphabetical order, not necessarily consecutively (e.g. abet but not able or abbey)

The program should be case insensitive, which means that characters should be converted to lower case before testing. The program should echo every word read, and follow the word (on the same line) with something like "MATCH -- three characters in strict alphabetic order" or "MATCH -- all letters in alphabetic order" for words which satisfy either condition.

Thus, given the input:	The output might appear:
abort	abort MATCH -- all characters in alphabetic order.
alphabetic	alphabetic
astute	astute MATCH -- three characters in sequence.
broccoli	broccoli
devious	devious

It might be fun to redirect the system file /usr/dict/words (which is the spelling check dictionary) to your standard input, and pipe the output to grep MATCH (which prints only those lines containing "MATCH"). The command line for this would be

yourprogname </usr/dict/words | grep MATCH.

(But PLEASE don't print out the file /usr/dict/words -- it would be about 500 pages.)

The program should be implemented using C constructs we have studied so far. Character arrays or pointers are not required.

The end of the input will be indicated by end-of-file. This is indicated by a value of EOF (which is defined in <stdio.h> to be -1) returned by either getchar() or scanf(). In testing your program with keyboard input, an end-of-file can be input be typing control-D.

Hints:
Read and write the input character-by-character, using "boolean variables" to record appropriate logical conditions. The end of each word will be marked by the newline character, '\n'.

You may assume that the end-of-file will always occur immediately after a newline (this is a unix convention); i.e. you won't have end-of-file in the middle of a word.

PROGRAMMING PROJECT 5-2

Purpose: character processing, more practice with functions.

Write a program to translate input text into pig latin. The translation can be done character-by character, without using string variables. The program skips non-alphabetic characters until it comes to an alphabetic character, which will be the first character of a word. If this character is a vowel ('a', 'e', 'i', 'o', or 'u'), it reads and wwrites out the word with the end. If the first character of the word is not a vowel, it writes out the word without its first character, and adds the original first character of the word plus 'ay' at the end. Any blanks and punctuation marks should not be counted as part of a word, but should be written just as they are read. The program continues until an end of file is read. A sample run, with input in boldface, is shown below:

```
Language translator program; enter lines of text:
```
pray to heaven, but row to shore!

```
raypay otay eavenhay, utbay owray otay horesay!
```

<cntrl-d>

Use the principles of tow-down design described in the previous chapter. You will probably find it useful to write the following functions as part of your program:

Skip_Non_Word() -- reads and writes blanks and punctuation marks, and returns the first alphabetic character it finds.

Read_Word() -- reads and writes alphabetic characters, and returns the first non-alphabetic character it finds.

Is_Vowel(Ch) -- returns 1 if the character is a vowel, and 0 otherwise.

Make sure your code handles end-of-file gracefully (i.e. without crashingor getting stuck in a loop).

CHAPTER 6

THE ARITHMETIC DATA TYPES

Although the chapter title is "arithmetic data types", it is as much about the different sizes and formats of variables that the computer manipulates. Details of the binary representation of a number are not introduced until chapter 7, but it helps describe it briefly here to explain the difference between unsigned and signed variables.

- Show the different storage formats for variables, and organize the various data types according to size, signed vs. unsigned, and integer vs. floating representations. Then, to reduce the confusion, emphasize that most of the time `int`, `float`, `double`, and `char` are the types that will be used.

- Go over the rules for mixing data types in an expression -- numerous examples can be presented in class.

- Some discussion should be devoted to the special issues involving floating types -- inexact representation, round-off error, and loss of precision. A detailed study of this is material for a course in itself, but students should be made aware of the potential for problems. They are always impressed by seeing a result they know should be 6.00000 get printed out as 5.99999.

- The math library is much too large to expect the students to know every function, but they should be given a general idea of what is available and how to find out more about it. In a unix environment, I encourage students to make use of *man math*.

TRANSPARENCY MASTERS

The arithmetic data types
Binary vs. decimal numbers
The floating types and scientific notation
Mathematical functions and the math library
Mixing types in expressions
An example: computing interest

ANSWERS TO EXERCISES

1. The initializer for "y" as shown in the exercise must have the last five digits zero in order for the two numbers to be distinct. This is because a "double" type has 15 to 16 decimal places of precision (both to the left and to the right of the decimal point); any additional precision cannot be represented in a "double".

2. The following program will determine whether printf rounds or truncates. (It rounds.)

```
#include <stdio.h>

main ()
{
    printf("The number 3.777 is printed out as %lf", 3.777);
    printf(" in two decimal places.\n");
}
```

5. The following program prints out a table of trigonometric values.

```
/*  Program to print a table of sin, cos, and tan.
 */

#define   PI      3.14159
#define   INCREMENT      PI/20.0

#include <stdio.h>
#include <math.h>

main ()
{
    double Angle;

    printf("\n\nTable of trigometric functions\n");
    printf("(angles in radians):\n\n");
    printf("%11s%18s%15s%15s\n",
           "X:", "sin(X):", "cos(X):", "tan(X):");

    for (Angle = 0.0 ; Angle <= PI ; Angle += INCREMENT)
       printf("%12.2lf   %12.2lf   %12.2lf   %12.2lf\n",
              Angle, sin(Angle), cos(Angle), tan(Angle));
}
```

6. On a 16-bit machine, the following output is produced:

```
i with %d format is -1536
u with %d format is -1536
i with %u format is 64000
u with %u format is 64000
```

The number 64000 is greater than the maximum positive value which can be stored in an int on a 16-bit machine. The value has overflowed into the sign bit, which causes it to appear negative when printed in a signed format.

8. The following program prints a table of square and fourth roots.

```
/* Program to print a table of square and fourth roots
 */

#define    MAX   100

#include <stdio.h>
#include <math.h>

main ()
{
    int    i;
    double Square_root, Fourth_root;

    printf("\n\n%7s%24s%24s\n", "Integer",
            "Square root", "Fourth root");
    for (i = 1 ; i <= MAX ; i++)   {
        Square_root = sqrt( (double) i);
        Fourth_root = sqrt(Square_root);
        printf("%7d%24lf%24lf\n", i,
                Square_root, Fourth_root);
    }
}
```

11. The only function which is changed is compute. If the variable nyears were not cast as a double, then assuming that ANSI style function prototype for pow is in the *math.h* include file, the type will be converted automatically by the compiler, and there will be no difference in the output.

```
#include <math.h>

double compute (double principal, double rate, int nyrs)
{
    rate *= 0.01;  /* convert e.g. 7% to 0.07 */
    return  principal * pow(rate, (double) nyrs);
}
```

12. The following program will be of use to those with large amounts of money to invest:

```c
/* Program to compare various investment strategies.
 * Inputs the amount to invest, in dollars
 * Prints out the amount resulting after 10 and 20 years,
 * for each of the following choices:
 *      9% compounded yearly,
 *      8.75% compounded quarterly,
 *      and 8.7% compounded daily.
 */
#include <stdio.h>
#include <math.h>

double find_accrued_interest (
     double principal,
     double rate,     /* interest rate */
     double c_rate,   /* compounding rate */
     double period    /* in years */
     )
{
     return principal * power(1.0 + rate, c_rate * period);
}

/* Check interest options for a given number of years */
void compare_interest_options (double principal, int nyears)
{
     printf("\n----- %d year investments -----\n", nyears);
     printf("9%% compounded yearly: $%.2f\n",
          find_accrued_interest(principal, 0.09, 1.0,
                         (double) nyears));
     printf("8.75%% compounded quarterly: $%.2f\n",
          find_accrued_interest(principal, 0.0875, 4.0,
                         (double) nyears));
     printf("8.7%% compounded daily: $%.2f\n",
          find_accrued_interest(principal, 0.087, 365.0,
                         (double) nyears));
}

main ()
{
     double    principal;

     printf("Investment advising program.\n");
     printf("Enter amount you have to invest:  ");
     scanf("%lf", &principal);

     compare_interest_options(principal, 10);
     compare_interest_optiona(principal, 20);
}
```

13. On most systems, the code shown will print `4294967295`, the largest possible unsigned integer. The reason is that in the two's complement representation for signed integers, -1 is represented by a word with all bits "1". This is the same as the representation for the largest possible integer for unsigned integers. Note that assigning a negative number to an unsigned variable is a form of overflow.

14. The following is an integer power function. Note that the exponent must be an integer, but the base is a double.

```
double i_power (double Base, int Exponent)
{
        double    product = 1.0;
        int   i;

        for (i = 1 ; i <= Exponent ; ++i)
            product *= Base;
        return product;
}
```

15. On most systems, the code shown will print out a value of zero. In general, when a value which is too big is assigned to a char variable, the actual value assigned is the low-order byte, or the value mod 256.

17. On most 16-bit systems, the code will produce the following output:

```
sizeof(c) = 1
sizeof('a')    = 2
sizeof(c = 'a')     = 2
sizeof(a + b + 7.7) = 8
```

On most 32-bit systems, the code will produce the following output:

```
sizeof(c) = 1
sizeof('a')    = 4
sizeof(c = 'a')     = 4
sizeof(a + b + 7.7) = 8
```

18. On a 16-bit system, the following output will be produced:

```
The largest unsigned int is 65535

65535 + 0 = 65535
65535 + 1 = 0
65535 + 2 = 1
65535 + 3 = 2
65535 + 4 = 3
65535 + 5 = 4
65535 + 6 = 5
65535 + 7 = 6
65535 + 8 = 7
65535 + 9 = 8
65535 * 0 = 0
65535 * 1 = 65535
65535 * 2 = 65534
65535 * 3 = 65533
65535 * 4 = 65532
65535 * 5 = 65531
65535 * 6 = 65530
65535 * 7 = 65529
65535 * 8 = 65528
65535 * 9 = 65527
```

The arithmetic is being done "modulo 65536", the largest unsigned integer plus one. Results wrap around from 65535 to 0.

21. The program below computes "pow(x, x)". On our system, 146 is the largest integer value for X which yields an accurate result. On at least one 16-bit microcomputer, 26 is the largest integer which yields an accurate result.

```
#include <math.h>

main ()
{
    double X;

    printf("Enter a floating number:  ");
    scanf("%lf", &X);
    printf("X = %lf and pow(X, X) = %lf.\n",
                        X, pow(X, X));
}
```

23. Here is the completed program:

```
/* Print a table of decimal, hexadecimal,
 * and octal integers
 */
#define    LIMIT       100

main ()
{
    int  i;

    printf("%12s%12s%12s\n",
            "decimal", "hex", "octal");
    printf("    --------    --------    --------\n");
    for (i = 0 ; i <= LIMIT ; ++i)
        printf("%12d%12x%12o\n", i, i, i);
}
```

Here is the first few lines of output from the program:

```
Table of decimal, hexadecimal, and octal values.
        decimal         hex         octal
        --------    --------    --------
            0           0           0
            1           1           1
            2           2           2
            3           3           3
            4           4           4
            5           5           5
            6           6           6
            7           7           7
            8           8          10
            9           9          11
           10           A          12
           11           B          13
           12           C          14
           13           D          15
           14           E          16
           15           F          17
           16          10          20
           17          11          21
           18          12          22
```

24. The following program compares the two numbers.

```
/* Program to compare pi to the e power
 * and e to the pi power.
 */

#include <stdio.h>
#include <math.h>

#define    PI    3.14159
#define    E     2.71828

main ()
{
      double    pi_to_the_e, e_to_the_pi;

      pi_to_the_e = power(PI, E);
      e_to_the_pi = power(E, PI);

      printf("pi raised to the e power is %lf\n",
                  pi_to_the_e);
      printf("e raised to the pi power is %lf\n",
                  e_to_the_pi);

      if (pi_to_the_e > e_to_the_pi)
          printf("pi_to_the_e");
      else
          printf("e_to_the_pi");
      printf(" is larger.\n");
}
```

On our system, the the following output was produced:

```
pi raised to the e power is 22.459059
e raised to the pi power is 23.140582
e_to_the_pi is larger.
```

PROGRAMMING PROJECT 6-1

Purpose: looping and conditional control structures; simulation techniques.

Computer models are frequently used to simulate natural processes such as the growth of animal populations. Several mathematical models exist which describe population biology. In isolation, a given population P will grow exponentially over time, given by $P(t) = P0 \cdot e^{Rt}$, where $P0$ is the initial population and R is the growth rate. In practice however growth will be limited by food supply or some other resource, measured by the *carrying capacity* K of the environment. This yields the *logistic model*, $P(t) = P(t-1) + R \cdot P(t-1) \cdot (1 - P(t-1)/K)$. (In this case the population is computed as an increment over the population in the previous time step.) Often two (or more) populations $P1$ and $P2$ will compete for the same resources, and then their growth will be affected not only by their respective growth rates $R1$ and $R2$ and carying capacities $K1$ and $K2$ but also by the effect each has on the other's food supply, measured by the *competition coefficients* $C1$ and $C2$. This yields the *competition model*, given by:

$$P1(t) = P1(t-1) + R1 \cdot P1(t-1) \cdot (K1 - P1(t-1) - (C1 \cdot P2(t-1))) / K1$$

$$P2(t) = P2(t-1) + R2 \cdot P2(t-1) \cdot (K2 - P2(t-1) - (C2 \cdot P1(t-1))) / K2$$

You are to write a program to simulate the competition of two species as described by the above equations. The simulation will proceed in a series of discrete time steps (i.e. in a for-loop). The program begins by prompting the user for the following parameters:

    Initial population for species 1 (P1(0));
    Initial population for species 2 (P2(0));
    Growth rates for species 1 and 2 (R1 and R2);
    Carrying capacities for species 1 and 2 (K1 and K2) ;
    Competition coefficients for species 1 and 2 (C1 and C2).

At each time step the new values of $P1$ and $P2$ are computed in terms of the values at the previous time step, and the time step and the two population numbers are displayed. After the indicated number of time steps the program stops and again asks for a number of time steps to run. In this way you can continue for as long as desired. The end of the run is indicated by any non-numeric input for the number of time steps.

The populations should be represented as integers and the other parameters as floats. Most of the programming effort will be in the input checking so you should make sure to check for the following input conditions:

    All input values must be greater than zero;
    Growth rates should be no more than 10.0;
    Competition coefficients should be no more than 5.0.

(The last two conditions are arbitrary). It is permissible for the initial population values to be greater than the carrying capacity (in which case the population will quickly decline to the carrying capacity). If an input error occurs, the program should issue an error message and repeat the input.

PROGRAMMING PROJECT 6-2

Purpose: Numeric calculations, math library.

This program is to print out a table showing the position of the sun as it moves across the sky during one day. This might be used as a tool by solar architects, gardeners, etc. The sun's position in the sky is described by two angles, the *altitude*, which measures its height (90 degrees is directly overhead), and the *azimuth*, or compass bearing (0 degrees is due south). These angles depend on the latitude, date, and time, and are given by the following equations:

$$\sin(Altitude) = \cos(L) \cos(D) \cos(H) + \sin(L) \sin(D)$$
$$\sin(Azimuth) = \cos(D) \sin(H) / \cos(Altitude)$$

where L is the latitude, D is the *declination* (measuring how far above or below the equator the sun is, based on the date), and H is the *hour angle* (measuring how far below the noon position the sun is based on the time):

$$D = 23.5 \sin(\# \ of \ days \ from \ March \ 21)$$
$$H = 0.25 \ \dot{} \ (\# \ of \ minutes \ from \ noon)$$

(The above equations are from "Solar Home Book" by Bruce Anderson, and have been simplified slightly). The sin and cos functions are in the standard math library, which you get by #include-ing <math.h>. Note that the equations give the sine of the sun angles, so you will have to use the library function asin (arcsin or inverse sine) to solve for the angles themselves. You will will also have to write functions to convert between radians and angles. The library functions sin, cos, and asin all use radians; however the latitude is input to the program in degrees, and the formulas for the declination and hour angle above use degrees. The conversion is given by:

$$Radians = \pi \ \dot{} \ Degrees \ / \ 180$$

The program is to input the latitude and number of days from March 21 (spring equinox), and then print out a table giving the sun's altitude and azimuth at each time in half-hour increments. The equations above will yield a negative altitude before sunrise and after sunset; your program should skip these and only print out sun angles for times when the sun is actually up.

If you are ambitious, you could modify the program to input the month and date, and calculate the number of days from March 21 and the current date. This is fairly easy using a switch statement to give the number of days in each month (ignore leap years).

CHAPTER 7

ENUMERATION TYPES AND BITWISE OPERATORS

This chapter could conceivably be skipped if time is limited. Non computer science majors, in particular, might never have use for the bitwise operators, although computer science majors will eventually find the topic essential.

- The basic concept of "user defiend types" as another form of structured programming. I don't try to "hide" the implementation of enumerated types behind a wall of formality -- they are much easier to understand if the student realizes that they are really just another form of integer. But at the same time, point out how their use makes the program self documenting and less prone to errors.

- The two's complement representation for signed number representation, and the differences (in more detail than the previous chapter) between signed and unsigned data types.

This is also a good time to describe in detail the difference between binary (base 2) representation and decimal (base 10) representation. I am always surprised at how many students lack a basic understanding of our base 10 number system; contrasting it with base 2, as well as base 8 (octal) and base 16 (hexadecimal) will put it into perspective. I like to present the "binary to decimal" and "decimal to binary" conversion algorithms as class examples, even though this is done automatically by `printf`. It always helps to give students an awareness of what is going on "behind the scenes".

TRANSPARENCY MASTERS

Enumeration type specifiers and `typedef`
Example: *find_next_day* program
Example: *paper, rock, and scissors* (summary)
Two's complement representation
Bitwise and shifting operators
Examples of bitwise operations
Operator precedence and associativity
Example: *bit_print*
Example: packing and unpacking bytes

ANSWERS TO EXERCISES

1. Shown below is an enumeration type for the months of the year, a function that yields the previous month for a given month, and a program that exercises it.

```
/* type definitions for months */
enum month {jan,feb,mar,apr,may,jun,jul,aug,sep,oct,nov,dec};
typedef   enum month     month;

/* function to return previous month, dec yields jan */
month previous_month (month M)
{
    switch (M) {
    case jan:
        M = dec; break;
    case feb:
        M = jan; break;
    case mar:
        M = feb; break;
    case apr:
        M = mar; break;
    case may:
        M = apr; break;
    case jun:
        M = may; break;
    case jul:
        M = jun; break;
    case aug:
        M = jul; break;
    case sep:
        M = aug; break;
    case oct:
        M = sep; break;
    case nov:
        M = oct; break;
    case dec:
        M = nov; break;
    }
    return  M;
}
```

```
void print_month (month M)
{
    switch (M)  {
    case jan:
        printf("January"); break;
    case feb:
        printf("February"); break;
    case mar:
        printf("March"); break;
    case apr:
        printf("April"); break;
    case may:
        printf("May"); break;
    case jun:
        printf("June"); break;
    case jul:
        printf("July"); break;
    case aug:
        printf("August"); break;
    case sep:
        printf("September"); break;
    case oct:
        printf("October"); break;
    case nov:
        printf("November"); break;
    case dec:
        printf("December"); break;
    }
}

main ()
{
    month M;

    printf("Table of months and their predecessors\n");
    printf("\n%16s%16s\n", "Month", "Predecessor");
    for (M = jan ; M <= dec ; M++)  {
        print_month(M);
        printf("        ");
        print_month(previous_month(M));
        putchar('\n');
    }
}
```

2.
```
/* Program to compute the next day/month from a given
 * day/month.  Uses the same enum definitions as exercise
 * 7-1, except that the integer values start at 1 instead
 * of 0 to correspond to common usage.
 */

#include <stdio.h>

enum        month        {jan=1, feb, mar, apr, may, jun, jul,
                          aug, sep, oct, nov, dec};
typedef  enum month        month;

/* Function to return the next month from a given month.
 * December wraps around to January
 */
month next_month (month M)
{
    switch (M)    {
    case jan:
       M = feb; break;
    case feb:
       M = mar; break;
    case mar:
       M = apr; break;
    case apr:
       M = may; break;
    case may:
       M = jun; break;
    case jun:
       M = jul; break;
    case jul:
       M = aug; break;
    case aug:
       M = sep; break;
    case sep:
       M = oct; break;
    case oct:
       M = nov; break;
    case nov:
       M = dec; break;
    case dec:
       M = jan; break;
    }
    return (M);
}
```

(2. continued)

```
/* Function to return the enum Month type
 *   corresponding to an integer 1-12
 */
month int_to_month (int Month_Num)
{
    return( (month) Month_Num);
}

/* Function to return the # of days in a given month.
 * Assumes February has 28 days.
 */
int Days_In_Month (month M)
{
    switch (M)   {
    case jan:
    case mar:
    case may:
    case jul:
    case aug:
    case oct:
    case dec:
        return 31;

    case apr:
    case jun:
    case sep:
    case nov:
        return 30;

    case feb:
        return 28;
    }
}
```

(2. continued)

```c
main ()
{
    /* re-used from the previous exercise: */
    void    print_month (month);

    month    Month;
    int      Month_Num, Day_Num, Date_OK = 0;

    printf("Enter a date in the form MM DD:  ");
    do {
        scanf("%d %d", &Month_Num, &Day_Num);
        if (Month_Num < 1 || Month_Num > 12)
            printf("Month must be between 1 and 12.");
        else {
            Month = int_to_month(Month_Num);
            if (Day_Num < 1 ||
                    Day_Num > Days_In_Month(Month))
                printf("Day is out of range.");
            else
                Date_OK = 1;
        }
    } while (! Date_OK);

    /* check for crossing to next month */
    if (Day_Num >= Days_In_Month(Month)) {
        Day_Num = 1;
        if (Month == dec)
            Month = jan;
        else
            Month = next_month(Month);
    }
    else
        ++Day_Num;

    /* print the date */
    printf("%d ", Day_Num);
    print_month(Month);
    putchar('\n');
}
```

3.

```
/* Progam to simulate a game of roulette.
 * All bets are $1, and the player starts with $10.
 * At each spin the player can enter a number between
 * 0 and 35 to bet on that number, the letter 'O' to
 * bet on any odd number, or the letter 'E' to bet on
 * any even number (except 0).
 */

/* enum definition for bet type
 * if the type is "number", a separate integer
 * gives the exact number bet on
 */
enum            bet_type  {odd, even, number, quit};
typedef         enum bet_type  bet_type;

/* Spin the roulette wheel;
 * return a pseudo random number between 0 and 35
 */
int Spin ()
{
    return rand() % 36;
}

/* Explain the betting options */
void prn_instructions ()
{
    printf("Enter: e  bet on any even number\n");
    printf("          (2-1 payoff)\n");
    printf("       o  bet on any odd number\n");
    printf("          (2-1 payoff)\n");
    printf("       n  bet on specific number\n");
    printf("          (35-1 payoff)\n");
    printf("       q  quit the prgoram\n");
}
```

(3. continued)

```
/* Get the bet type from the user */
bet_type Get_Bet ()
{
      char ch;

      printf("What kind of bet would you like to make? ");
      for (;;) {
            scanf(" %c", &ch);
            switch (ch) {
            case 'o':  case 'O':
                  return odd;
            case 'e':  case 'E':
                  return even;
            case 'n':  case 'N':
                  return number;
            case 'q':  case 'Q':
                  return quit;
            default:
                  prn_instructions();
            }
      }
}

/* Announce a win/loss */
int Win_Or_Lose (int Win, int Payoff)
{
      if (Win) {
            printf("Congratulaions! You win $%d.\n",
                        Payoff - 1);
            return(Payoff - 1);
      }
      else {
            printf("Too bad, you lose $1.\n");
            return(-1);
      }
}
```

(3. continued)

```
/* Compute the results of one bet
 * returns amount won/lost
 */
int Result (bet_type Bet_Type, int Bet_Number)
{
     int   Num;

     Num = Spin();
     printf("The number is ...... %d\n", Num);
     switch (Bet_Type) {
     case odd:
        return Win_Or_Lose(Num > 0 && Num % 2 == 1, 2);
     case even:
        return Win_Or_Lose(Num > 0 && Num % 2 == 0, 2);
     case number:
        return Win_Or_Lose(Num == Bet_Number, 35);
     }
}

main ()
{
     bet_type   bet;
     int        bet_number, amount = 10;

     printf("\nRoulette simulation program.\n");
     printf("You are given $10 to start.");
     printf("All bets are $1.\n");
     prn_instructions();

     while (amount > 0 && (bet = Get_Bet()) != quit) {
        if (bet == number) {
            printf("# to bet on: ");
            scanf("%d", &bet_number);
        }
        amount += Result(bet, bet_number);
        printf("\nYou now have $%d.\n", amount);
     }
     printf("...bye\n");
}
```

4. The balanced meal program is shown below. The number of different menus possible
is the product of the number of items in each group, in this case $4 \times 3 \times 4 \times 4 \times 4 = 768$.

```
/* Program to generate "balanced meals" by randomly
 * selecting one item from each of five basic food groups.
 * If the number of item in food group 1-5 is N1-N5,
 * then the number of distinct possible menus is
 * N1 * N2 * N3 * N4 * N5.
 */

#include <stdio.h>

enum fish {bass, salmon, shrimp, trout};
typedef   enum fish fish;
#define    NUM_FISH  4

enum fruit {apple, peach, pear};
typedef    enum fruit      fruit;
#define    NUM_FRUITS      3

enum grains {bread, oatmeal, rice, barley};
typedef     enum grains      grains;
#define     NUM_GRAINS       4

enum meats {steak, chicken, hamburger, turkey};
typedef    enum meats        meats;
#define    NUM_MEATS 4

enum vegetables {peas, broccoli, spinach, asparagus};
typedef    enum vegetables      vegetables;
#define    NUM_VEGETABLES 4

/* Print out the name of a fish, given an integer */
void print_fish (int Fish_Num)
{
    switch (Fish_Num)   {
    case 0:
       printf("bass"); break;
    case 1:
       printf("salmon"); break;
    case 2:
       printf("shrimp"); break;
    case 3:
       printf("trout"); break;
    }
}
```

(4. continued)

```c
/* Print the name of a fruit */
void print_fruit (int Fruit_Num)
{
    switch (Fruit_Num)   {
    case 0:
       printf("apple"); break;
    case 1:
       printf("peach"); break;
    case 2:
       printf("pear"); break;
    }
}

/* Print the name of a grain */
void print_grain (int Grain_Num)
{
    switch (Grain_Num)   {
    case 0:
       printf("bread"); break;
    case 1:
       printf("oatmeal"); break;
    case 2:
       printf("rice"); break;
    }
}

/* Print the name of a meat */
void print_meat (int Meat_Num)
{
    switch (Meat_Num)   {
    case 0:
       printf("Steak"); break;
    case 1:
       printf("chicken"); break;
    case 2:
       printf("hamburger"); break;
    case 3:
       printf("turkey"); break;
    }
}
```

(4. continued)

```c
/* Print the name of a vegetable */
void print_vegetable (int Vegetable_Num)
{
    switch (Vegetable_Num)  {
    case 0:
       printf("zucchini"); break;
    case 1:
       printf("peas"); break;
    case 2:
       printf("broccoli"); break;
    case 3:
       printf("spinach"); break;
    case 4:
       printf("asparagus"); break;
       }
}

main ()
{
    int    i;

    printf("Below are twenty randomly-generated");
    printf("pseudo-balanced menu plans\n\n");
    for (i = 1 ; i <= 20 ; i++)   {
       printf("\nMenu #%d:\n", i);
       print_fish(rand() % NUM_FISH);
       printf(", ");
       print_fruit( rand() % NUM_FRUITS);
       printf(", ");
       print_grain( rand() % NUM_GRAINS);
       printf(", ");
       print_meat( rand() % NUM_MEATS);
       printf(", ");
       print_vegetable( rand() % NUM_VEGETABLES);
       putchar('\n');
    }
}
```

5. To change the program so a more readable report is printed, the function report_result() is added, together with a function print_p_r_s to print out a value of the enumerated type.

```
/* The game of paper, rock, scissors. */

#include <stdio.h>
#include <ctype.h>
#include <stdlib.h>
#include <time.h>

enum p_r_s      {paper, rock, scissors, game, help,
                 instructions, quit};

enum outcome {win, lose, tie, error};

typedef    enum p_r_s      p_r_s;
typedef    enum outcome    outcome;

outcome    compare(p_r_s player, p_r_s machine);
void       game_status(int, int, int);
void       help_for_the_player (void);
void       prn_instructions(void);
p_r_s      selection_by_player(void);
p_r_s      selection_by_machine(void);
void report_result(p_r_s, p_r_s, outcome);

main ()
{
    int  win_cnt = 0, lose_cnt = 0, tie_cnt = 0;
    outcome    result;
    p_r_s      player, machine;

    srand(time(NULL));
    prn_instructions();
    while  ((player = selection_by_player()) != quit)
        switch (player) {
        case paper:
        case rock:
        case scissors:
            machine = selection_by_machine();
            result = compare(player, machine);
            if (result == win) {
                ++win_cnt;
                report_result(player, machine, result);
            }
            else if (result == lose) {
                ++lose_cnt;
                report_result(player, machine, result);
            }
```

(5. continued)

```
                    else if (result == tie) {
                        ++tie_cnt;
                        printf("A tie.\n");
                    }
                    break;
                case game:
                    game_status(win_cnt, lose_cnt, tie_cnt);
                    break;
                case instructions:
                    prn_instructions();
                    break;
                case help:
                    help_for_the_player();
                    break;
            }
        game_status(win_cnt, lose_cnt, tie_cnt);
        if (win_cnt > lose_cnt)
            printf("\nCONGRATULATIONS - You won!\n\n");
    }
/* print the name of "paper", "rock", or "scissors" */
void print_p_r_s (p_r_s choice)
{
    switch (choice)  {
    case paper:
        printf("paper");
        break;
    case rock:
        printf("rock");
        break;
    case scissors:
        printf("scissors");
        break;
    }
}
/* report the outcome of one round */
void report_result (p_r_s player, p_r_s machine,
                    outcome result)
{
    printf("You chose ");
    print_p_r_s(player);
    printf(" and I chose ");
    print_p_r_s(machine);
    printf(".  You ");
    if (result == win)
        printf("win.\n");
    else
        printf("lose.\n");
}
```

6. The second `typedef` is preferable, because it defines `false` as 0 and `true` as 1, which means for example that `if (true)` will work as expected (the statement following will be executed). The first typedef defines `false` as 1, which would yield unexpected results in situations such as `if (false)`.

7. The code to generate the bit pattern is as shown in the problem. The equivalent table of powers of ten will look the same except that the third column of numbers will have all 1's replaced by 9's.

8. The following code completes the outline in the problem. If the string contains more than 8 digits (or 4 digits for a 16-bit machine), all but the last 8 (or 4) digits will be lost.

```c
int convert (char *s)
{
    char   *p;
    int    a = 0;

    for (p = s ; *p != '\0' ; ++p)    {
        a <<= 4;
        switch (*p)   {
        case '1':
            a |= 1; break;
        case '2':
            a |= 2; break;
        case '3':
            a |= 3; break;
        case '4':
            a |= 4; break;
        case '5':
            a |= 5; break;
        case '6':
            a |= 6; break;
        case '7':
            a |= 7; break;
        case '8':
            a |= 8; break;
        case '9':
            a |= 9; break;
        case '0':
            break;
        }
    }
    return(a);
}
```

However, since both the ASCII and EBCDIC character codes have contiguous codes for the digits '0' through '9', the above can be simplified as follows:

```
int convert (char *s)
{
    int a = 0;

    while (*s != '\0')  {
        a <<= 4;
        a |= *s - '0';
        ++s;
    }
    return(a);
}
```

The following code takes an int and prints a string of 8 (for a 32-bit machine) or 4 (for a 16-bit machine) decimal digits.

```
/* Unpack binary coded decimal digits from an int.
 * The first digit packed will be rightmost in the int.
 * To avoid redundant shifting, we start with a shift
 * count equal to the size of an int in bits minus 4.
 * It is decreased by 4 for each digit until it is 0.
 */
void unconvert (int a)
{
    int     Shift = sizeof(int) * 8 - 4;
    char    Digit;

    for ( ; Shift >= 0 ; Shift -= 4) {
        /* First isolate the binary value
           for the current digit */
        Digit = (a >> Shift) & 0xF;
        /* to convert from the binary value of the digit
         * to the character code, we add the code for '0',
         * which works for both ASCII and EBCDIC
         */
        Digit += '0';
        putchar(Digit);
    }
    putchar('\n');
}
```

10.

Decimal number:	Binary for positive #:	Binary for negative #:
-1	0000000000000000	1111111111111111
-5	0000000000000101	1111111111111011
-101	0000000001100101	1111111110011011
-1023	0000001111111111	1111110000000001

11. The following function processes the bit strings right-to-left. At each step, it masks out all but the low-order bit position, and adds together the resulting 0 or 1. The result will be 2 or 3 if a majority of bits are 1. Unsigned types are used so that the sign bit is not propagated by the right shift.

```
short majority (unsigned short a, unsigned short b,
                unsigned short c)
{
    unsigned short   result = 0;
    int              i;

    for (i = 0 ; i < 16 ; i++)  {
        result >>= 1;
        if ( (a & 1) + (b & 1) + (c & 1) >= 2)
            result |= 0x8000;
        a >>= 1; b >>= 1; c >>= 1;
    }
    return(result);
}
```

The following is a simpler implementation which expresses the majority function as a logical operation on entire bit strings:

```
short maority (short a, short b, short c)
{
    return(a & b | b & c | a & c);
}
```

12. The following program implements a circular shift of bits.

```c
/* Program to demonstrate circular bit shifting */

/* The following function takes integers A and N,
 * and rotates A left by N bit positions.  Bits
 * shifted out the left are reintroduced at the right.
 */
int rotate_left (int A, int N)
{
    int Carry;

    while (N-- > 0)  {
        Carry = A & 0x80000000;
        A <<= 1;
        if (Carry)
            A++;
        }
    return(A);
}

/* The main program inputs an integer from the user
 * and calls rotate_left for shifts of 1, 2,... up to
 * 16, and prints out each result.  The last one
 * should be the same as the original number for 16-bit
 * machines. (For 32-bit machines, you have to rotate
 * 32 bit * positions to get back to the original
 * number.)
 */
main ()
{
    int A, i;
    void bit_print (int) ;    /*from text*/

    printf("Demonstrate circular bit shifting.\n");
    printf("Enter any integer:  ");
    scanf("%d", &A);

    printf("%20s%20s\n",
            "Positions rotated:", "Resulting value:");
    for (i = 1 ; i <= 16 ; i++)  {
        printf("%20d       ", i);
        bit_print( rotate_left(A, i) );
        putchar('\n');
    }
}
```

13.
```
/* Program to demonstrate reversing the bits in a number
 */
#include <stdio.h>
#include <limits.h>

/* The following function takes an int and returns
 * an int with reversed bits
 */
int flip_bits (int N)
{
    int     R = 0, i;
    int     bits_per_word = sizeof(int) * CHAR_BIT;

    for (i = 0 ; i < bits_per_word ; i++)  {
        R <<= 1;
        /* copy right bit of N into right bit of R */
        R |= N & 1;
        /* then shift R leftward and N rightward */
        N >>= 1;
    }
    return(R);
}

main ()
{
    int     N;

    printf("Enter an integer:  ");
    scanf("%d", &N);

    printf("The corresponding bit pattern is: ");
    bit_print(N);

    printf("\nAnd the reversed bit pattern is: ");
    bit_print( flip_bits(N) );
    printf("\n\n");
}
```

14. The following function extracts every other bit position from a 32-bit quantity into a 16-bit quantity. The variables are declared as `short` and `long` so it will work on any machine.

```
short  Extract (long L)
{
    int    i;
    short  S = 0;

    for (i = 0 ; i < 16 ; ++i) {
        S <<= 1;        /* next bit position in S */
        /* put highest bit of L into lowest bit of S */
        if ((L & 0x80000000L) != 0)
            ++S;
        L <<= 2;            /* next bit position in L */
    }
    return S;
}
```

15. When unsigned numbers are shifted right, zeroes are always shifted in at the left end. When signed negative numbers are shifted right, the value shifted in at the left end is machine-dependent. If the result of right shifting a signed negative number is the same as right shifting an unsigned number, it means that zeroes are being shifted in for a signed number, even though the sign bit would be one for a negative number.

16. The program below stores a date in a 16-bit integer.

```
/* Program to demonstrate packing a date into a
 * 16-bit quantity
 */

#include <stdio.h>

/* The following function takes a month, day, and year
 * as integers, and returns a 16 bit quantity
 * containing the month in the first 4 bits, the day
 * in the next 5 bits, and the year (0 - 99) in the
 * last 7 bits.
 */
short pack_date (int Month, int Day, int Year)
{
    /* make sure the year is 2 decimal digits */
    Year %= 100;
    return ( (Month << 12) | (Day << 7) | Year);
}
```

(16. continued)

```
    /* The following function takes a packed date in the
     * above format, unpacks the original month, day, and
     * year, and prints it out in the form MM/DD/YY.
     */
    void unpack_date (unsigned short D)
    {
        int     Month, Day, Year;
        /* mask out all but low 7 bits to get year */
        Year = D & 0x7F;
        /* shift the day into low-order bit positions */
        D >>= 7;
        /* mask out all but low 5 bits to get day */
        Day = D & 0x1F;
        /* shift the month into low-order bit positions */
        D >>= 5;
        Month = D;

        printf("%d/%d/%d\n", Month, Day, Year);
    }

    main ()
    {
        int     M, D, Y;
        short   packed_date;
        void    bit_print (int);

        printf("Program to demonstrate date packing.\n");
        printf("Enter a date in the form MM/DD/YY:    ");
        scanf("%d/%d/%d", &M, &D, &Y);

        packed_date = pack_date(M, D, Y);
        printf("\nThe packed bit pattern is:  ");
        bit_print(packed_date);

        printf("\nAnd unpacking the date again yields:  ");
        unpack_date(packed_date);
    }
```

17. The function below acts directly on a packed date to produce the next date. The function calls the `Days_In_Month` function from exercise 2, but it is omitted from the listing below to save space.

```
/* Function to change a date packed in a 16-bit integer
 * into the next calendar date.  The format is the same
 * as exercise 16: the month is in the first 4 bits, the
 * day is in the next 5 bits, and the year (0 - 99)
 * is in the last 7 bits.
 */
short Next_Date (unsigned short Date)
{
    /* Mask the date field and compare with the number
     * of days in the month, appropriately shifted
     */
    if ((Date & 0xF80) >= (Days_In_Month(Date >> 12) << 7)) {

        /* If into next month, reset date field */
        Date &= 0xF07F;

        /* and increment the month */
        Date += 1 << 12;

        /* check for past end of year */
        if ((Date & 0xF000) > (12 << 12)) {

            /* if past end of year, set month to one */
            Date &= 0x0FFF;
            Date |= 0x1000;

            /* and increment the year */
            ++Date;
        }
    }
    /* increment date field */
    Date += 1 << 7;
    return Date;
}
```

18. The following program generates a boolean truth table using bit values.

```
/* Print a table of values for some boolean functions.
 * Uses bitwise representation for the boolean values
 * in the low-order 5 bits of the char variable B
 */
#include <stdio.h>

/* Definitions of bit masks for the 5 boolean values */
#define        B1    16
#define        B2    8
#define        B3    4
#define        B4    2
#define        B5    1
```

(18. continued)

```
main ()
{
  char      b;     /* represents all boolean variables */
  int       cnt = 0 ;

  printf("\n%5s%5s%5s%5s%5s%5s%7s%7s%11s\n\n",
      "Cnt", "b1", "b2", "b3", "b4", "b5",
      "fct1", "fct2", "majority");

  /* do-loops are used instead of for-loops as
   * we need the condition ckecked at the end.
   */
  b = 0;
  do {
    do {
      do {
        do {
          do {
            printf("%5d%5d%5d%5d%5d%5d%6d%7d%9d\n",
                /* Here !! is used to convert a bit
                 * to zero or one.
                 */
                ++cnt,
              !! (b & B1),
              !! (b & B2),
              !! (b & B3),
                 !! (b & B4),
              !! (b & B5),
                /* Note || and && still used instead
             * of * | and &, since we are using
             * boolean value of a bit != 0.
                 */
                (b & B1) || (b & B3) || (b & B5),
                (b & B1) && (b & B2)
               || (b & B4) && (b & B5),
                !!(b & B1) + !!(b & B2) + !!(b & B3)
                  + !!(b & B4) + !!(b & B5) >= 3);
                b ^= B5;          /* flip the bit */
              } while (b & B5) ; /* loop if it's 1 */
              b ^= B4;
            } while (b & B4) ;
            b ^= B3;
          } while (b & B3) ;
          b ^= B2;
        } while (b & B2);
        b ^= B1;
  } while (b & B1);
  printf ("\n");
}
```

19. Here is a version of the program above using machine arithmetic to simplify changing the bit values.

```
/* Print a table of values for some boolean functions.
 * Uses bitwise representation for the boolean values
 * in the low-order 5 bits of the char variable B
 * Takes advantage of machine arithmetic by "counting"
 * the boolean values.
 */
#include <stdio.h>

/* Definitions for bit masks for the 5 boolean values */
#define      B1      16
#define      B2      8
#define      B3      4
#define      B4      2
#define      B5      1

main ()
{
     char b;    /* represents all boolean variables */
     int  cnt = 0 ;

     printf("\n%5s%5s%5s%5s%5s%5s%7s%7s%11s\n\n",
          "Cnt", "b1", "b2", "b3", "b4", "b5",
          "fct1", "fct2", "majority");

     for (b = 0 ; b < 32 ; ++b)
          printf("%5d%5d%5d%5d%5d%5d%6d%7d%9d\n",
               /* instead of a separate counter variable
                * just use b itself
                */
               b + 1,
               /* Here !! is used to convert a bit
                * to zero or one.
                */
                    !! (b & B1), !! (b & B2), !! (b & B3),
               !! (b & B4), !! (b & B5),
               /* Note || and && still used instead of
                * | and &, since we are using boolean
                * value of a bit != 0.
                */
               (b & B1) || (b & B3) || (b & B5),
               (b & B1) && (b & B2) || (b & B4) && (b & B5),
               !! (b & B1) + !! (b & B2) + !! (b & B3)
                    + !! (b & B4) + !! (b & B5) >= 3);
     printf ("\n");
}
```

20. The following program shows the bit patterns for N, $N \times 2$, $N \times 4$, and $N \times 8$. The bit pattern is shifted one bit to the left for each factor of 2.

```
/* Program to demonstrate that 2*N is the same as N<<1,
 * 4 * N is the same  as N << 2,
 * and 8 * N is the same as N << 3
 * (providing that overflow does not occur).
 */

#include <stdio.h>

main ()
{
    int    N;
    void   bit_print(int);

    printf("Enter an integer: ");
    scanf("%d", &N);
    printf("\nBit pattern for N:      ");
    bit_print(N);
    printf("\nBit pattern for 2 * N:  ");
    bit_print(2 * N);
    printf("\nBit pattern for 4 * N:  ");
    bit_print(4 * N);
    printf("\nBit pattern for 8 * N:  ");
    bit_print(8 * N);
    printf("\n\n");
}
```

21. If -a is the same as ~a + 1 , then ~a is the same as -a - 1.

```
int bit_complement (int N)
{
    return(-N - 1);
}
```

22. The following function packs four chars into a 32-bit "int" using a single expression.

```
#include <limits.h>

int pack (char a, char b, char c, char d)
{
    return( ( (a << CHAR_BIT | b) << CHAR_BIT | c)
               << CHAR_BIT | d);
}
```

23. The above is rewritten using only arithmetic operators by substituting + for |
(which works because zeroes are shifted in at the right on a left shift), and substituting *
256 for << CHAR_BIT.

```
int pack (char a, char b, char c, char d)
{
    return( ( (a * 256 + b) * 256 + c) * 256 + d);
}
```

25. EOF is defined to be -1 in *stdio.h*. The bit pattern for -1 is the same as the bit
pattern for 255 for an unsigned char. If a plain char is implemented as an
unsigned char, then it will be promoted to unsigned int in a comparison, and
therefore will have the value 255, which is different from EOF (which is -1).

26. The ASCII character codes for 'a', 'b', and 'c' are 97, 98, and 99, respectively. The
output shown is the bit pattern for these values. Note that on the Sun workstation, as on
many computers, multi-character constants are stored in a word with the first character in
the low-order position, i.e. backwards.

CHAPTER 8

FUNCTIONS AND POINTERS

With this chapter begins the study of what is one of the great strengths of C, and at the same time one of the things that makes it more difficult than other languages to master. Other languages have pointers, but they do not match the range of what you can do with pointers in C. The coverage of pointers is broken up over three chapters to ease this process, so students should not be expected to know all about pointers right away.

- Spend some time on the basic concept of pointers. Rather than "hiding" the real nature of pointers as addresses, as is sometimes done in more formal approaches, I believe it gives the students a better intuitive grasp of what is going on to introduce pointers in terms of machine addresses. At the beginning, I even use actual numeric addresses in class examples (this is also done in the text). This is an entirely new concept for most students, so I use numerous simple exaples.

- This is a case where "a picture is worth a thousand words". Every example involving pointers should be accompanied by a blackboard diagram showing the pointer values as arrows.

- Show some of the problems which can arise using pointers -- aliasing, for example, and the difference between pointer assignments and data assignments.

- Emphasize the necessity of initializing a pointer before using it, and the difference between initializing a pointer and initializing the data to which it points. Show some of the errors resulting from pointer errors. On many computers this shows up as a "segment fault" or "bus error", which can sound quite intimidating if they have not seen it before.

- Many compilers allow an integer to be used where a pointer is supposed to occur, with only a warning message. Make sure students understand that this is rarely going to work at run-time, and that a cast will shut the compiler up but will not correct the problem.

- Call by reference is both an example of the use of pointers and an important topic in its own right. In particular, this is the time for all those examples you couldn't use in previous chapters because they involved a function which returned more than one value to the caller.

● Storage classes are a separate topic from pointers, and are another topic that many students find difficult. It helps to show the most commonly used cases (static variables in a function, and external variables for programs built in several modules), rather than just presenting the storage classes in their complete generality.

I wouldn't spend too much time on the "pointer to a pointer to a pointer ..." examples. It's nice to illustrate the theoretical generality, but they are not very useful in practice. I have found that too much emphasis on the esoteric only convinces some students that they never will understand pointers.

TRANSPARENCY MASTERS

Pointers #1
Pointers #2
Pointers #3
Pointers #4
Call by reference
Scope rules
`extern` storage class
`register` storage class
`static` storage class
Static external variables
Example: character processing

ANSWERS TO EXERCISES

1. The output is the following:

     NNN   7   5   15   9

where NNN is the address at which variable `i` is located.

2. Below are shown the statements and declarations and the contents of memory after each step:

```
char c1 = 'A', c2 = 'B', tmp;
char *p = &c1, *q = &c2;
```

c1: [A] c2: [B] tmp: [?] p: [&c1] q: [&c2]

```
tmp = *p;
```

c1: [A] c2: [B] tmp: [A] p: [&c1] q: [&c2]

```
*p = *q;
```

c1: [B] c2: [B] tmp: [A] p: [&c1] q: [&c2]

```
*q = tmp;
```

c1: [B] c2: [A] tmp: [A] p: [&c1] q: [&c2]

3. The only integer value which may be assigned to a pointer is zero. The second statement is accepted because 7 - 5 - 2 = 0. Changing the pointer types to `int *` won't make the compiler happy.

4.

`p = &i`	legal.
`*q = &j`	illegal; left side is type "int", right side is type "* int".
`p = &*&i`	illegal; cannot take address of expression "*&i".
`i = (*&) j`	illegal; (*&) is meaningless.
`i = (int) p`	legal.
`i = *&*&j`	illegal; cannot take address of expression *&*&j.
`q = &p`	illegal; left side is type "*int" but right side is type "**int"
`i = (*p)++ + *q`	legal.

5. In general, we can deduce how many bytes are allocated to the variables by the difference between their addresses, although this is not guaranteed. The following program prints out the variables' addresses:

```
main ()
{
    char    a, b, c, *p, *q, *r;

    printf("&a is %p, &b is %p, ", &a, &b);
    printf("&c is %p, &p is %p, ", &c, &p);
    printf("&q is %p, and &r is %p.\n", &q, &r);
}
```

6. The program below circularly shifts five character variables using pointers.

```
/* Program to demonstrate circular shifting of five
 * character variables
 */

#include <stdio.h>

/* The following function replaces the values of
 *    *p1, *p2, *p3, *p4, and *p5
 * by the values of *p2, *p3, *p4, *p5, and *p1.
 */
void shift (char *p1,
            char *p2,
        char *p3,
        char *p4,
        char *p5)
{
    char    temp = *p1;

    *p1 = *p2;
    *p2 = *p3;
    *p3 = *p4;
    *p4 = *p5;
    *p5 = temp;
}

main ()
{
    char    c1, c2, c3, c4, c5;
    int     i;

    printf("Please enter five charcters:  ");
    scanf("%c%c%c%c%c", &c1, &c2, &c3, &c4, &c5);

    printf("Here are your characters, ");
    printf("circularly shifted five times:\n");
    for (i = 1 ; i <= 5 ; i++)  {
        shift(&c1, &c2, &c3, &c4, &c5);
        printf("%c %c %c %c %c\n", c1, c2, c3, c4, c5);
    }
}
```

7. The following program orders 3 characters using call by reference.

```c
/* Demonstrate sorting 3 char variables
 * using call by reference
 */
#include <stdio.h>

/* Function to exchange 2 char variables */
void swap (char *cp1, char *cp2)
{
    char temp;

    temp = *cp1;
    *cp1 = *cp2;
    *cp2 = temp;
}

/* Function to order 3 char variables */
void order (char *cp1, char *cp2, char *cp3)
{
    /* First get the larger of cp1 and cp2 into cp2 */
    if (*cp1 > *cp2)
        swap(cp1, cp2);

    /* Next get the largest of the three into cp3 */
    if (*cp2 > *cp3)
        swap(cp2, cp3);

    /* Now get the second largest into cp2 */
    if (*cp1 > *cp2)
        swap(cp1, cp2);
}

main ()
{
    char c1, c2, c3;

    printf("Sort 3 characters using pointers.\n");
    printf("Enter 3 characters, or EOF to quit.\n");
    for (;;) {
        putchar('>');
        if (scanf(" %c%c%c", &c1, &c2, &c3) == EOF)
            exit(0);
        order(&c1, &c2, &c3);
        printf("In ascending order: %c %c %c\n",
            c1, c2, c3);
    }
}
```

8. The following is the "process characters" program without pointers.

```
/* Process some characters without using pointers */
#include <stdio.h>
#include <ctype.h>

#define    NWORDS    3

main ()
{
    int   c, nchars = 0, nletters = 0,
          last_char = ' ', cnt = 0;

    while ((c = getchar()) != EOF)   {
        if (! isspace(last_char) || ! isspace(c)) {
            if (isalpha(c)) {
                ++nletters;
                if (islower(c))
                    c = toupper(c);
            }
            else if (isspace(c))
                if (++cnt % NWORDS == 0)
                    c = '\n';
                else
                    c = ' ';
            ++nchars;
            last_char = c;
            putchar(c);
        }
    }
    printf("\n%s%5d\n%s%5d\n\n",
        "Number of characters:", nchars,
        "Number of letters:   ", nletters);
}
```

9. The following program unpacks all four bytes from a long using call by reference.

```c
#include <stdio.h>
#include <limits.h>

/* Unpack the packed int p into 4 characters. */
void unpack (int p, char *pa, char *pb,
                char *pc, char *pd)
{
    unsigned    mask = 255;   /* start at low byte */

    *pa = p & mask;
    p >>= CHAR_BIT;
    *pb = p & mask;
    p >>= CHAR_BIT;
    *pc = p & mask;
    p >>= CHAR_BIT;
    *pd = p & mask;
}

main ()
{
    int     N;
    char    a, b, c, d;
    void    bit_print (int);

    printf("Enter an integer:  ");
    scanf("%d", &N);

    unpack(N, &a, &b, &c, &d);
    printf("Here is the bit pattern for N:  ");
    bit_print(N);
    printf("\nand here are the bit patterns ");
    printf("for the four unpacked chars:\n");
    bit_print(a);
    putchar('\n');
    bit_print(b);
    putchar('\n');
    bit_print(c);
    putchar('\n');
    bit_print(d);
    putchar('\n');
}
```

10. On most systems, a pointer is stored in four bytes. It should not take any more space to store a pointer to a "long double" than a pointer to a "char". The following program verifies this.

```
main ()
{
    char    A, *PA;
    short   B, *PB;
    int     C, *PC;
    long    D, *PD;
    float   E, *PE;
    double  F, *PF;

    printf("Pointer to:    Size of pointer in bytes:\n");
    printf("%15s%10d\n", "char", sizeof(PA));
    printf("%15s%10d\n", "short", sizeof(PB));
    printf("%15s%10d\n", "int", sizeof(PC));
    printf("%15s%10d\n", "long", sizeof(PD));
    printf("%15s%10d\n", "float", sizeof(PE));
    printf("%15s%10d\n", "double", sizeof(PF));
}
```

11. As written, the code produces the following output:

```
48
63
```

If all the blanks in the two expressions are removed, the output is the following:

```
64
45
```

If all blanks around binary expressions are retained but other blanks are removed, the output is the following:

```
63
64
```

12. The initializer:

```
int  *p = LUCKY_NUMBER;
```

assigns to p the value of LUCKY_NUMBER, not the address of LUCKY_NUMBER. (It's illegal to take the address of a constant anyway.) Therefore the printf statement prints out the contents of whatever is stored at location 777 (which is probably not your lucky number).

13. The expression q == &p does make sense, since both q and &p are of type pointer to pointer to int. The expression tests whether q contains the address of the variable p.

14. The value 7 appears three times because the variable v is referenced three times: once via *&v , once via **&p (which is equal to *p), and once via ***&q (which is equal to **q). The address of v appears three times, once as &v , once as *&p (which is equal to p), and once as **&q (which is equal to *q). The address of p appears twice, once as &p and once as *&q (which is equal to q).

The construct & * would be meaningful before a pointer or address expression.

16. If you want to declare a static external variable, place the declaration outside of any function, which automatically makes it external, and use the storage class static, e.g.:

```
#include <stdio.h>

static     int  a = 1;

main ()
   ...
```

17. We can keep the const and also keep the compiler happy by doing away with the pointer altogether. It complains because by assigning the address of a const variable to a pointer, it is no longer possible to ensure that the variable is not changed.

```
const      float    x = 7.7;

printf("x = %g\n", x);
```

PROGRAMMING PROJECT 8-1

Purpose: More practice with functions; call by reference using addresses.

Write a program to compute the exact number of days between any two dates in history. A sample run, with user input in boldface, would be:

```
Enter first date: 10/5/1846
Enter second date: 6/2/2005
There are 57949 days between the two dates.
```

Note that the year must be entered as four digits since it can be from any century. (For this assignment you can ignore the fact that different calendars have been used in different periods in history, and just extend the calendar we currently use forward and backward in time.) The program should check the input format for each date, including: presence of '/' between numbers, month between 1 and 12, and date within the actual number of days for that month. If an input error occurs the program should print an appropriate message and re-input the date. Use the following rule to compute leap years:

Any year which is a multiple of 4 is a leap year;
unless it's also a multiple of 100, in which case it's not a leap year;
unless it's also a multiple of 400, in which case it is a leap year.

For example, 1800 is not a leap year, but 1600 is a leap year.

Hints: For dates in different years, you could use the following stepwise refinement:

(# of days from first date to Dec. 31 of same year)
+ 365 * (# of intervening leap years)
+ (1 for each leap year between the two years)
+ (# of days from Jan. 1 of last year to last date)
+ 1.

The following functions will be useful:

A function which reads in a date, checks for input errors, and returns (using call-by-reference) the month, day, and year;

A function which takes as a parameter a month number and a year and returns the actual number of days in that month, using a switch statement on the month number (it needs to know the year also as February has 29 days in leap years);

A boolean function which takes a year and returns 1 if it is a leap year and 0 otherwise;

A function which gives the number of days between two dates in the same year (it doesn't have to know the exact year but it does have to know if it's a leap year).

PROGRAMMING PROJECT 8-2

Purpose: Call-by-reference using pointer parameters;
more practice with top-down design using functions.

For this assignment you are to write a program to compute the local maxima or minima of a third-degree (cubic) polynomial, using the algebraic method described here. A cubic polynomial of the form

$$Ax^3 + Bx^2 + Cx + D$$

is defined by the four coefficients $A, B, C,$ and D; therefore to represent the polynomial in a computer program you just need four variables for the four coefficients. To find the local maxima and minima, you first find the derivative of the polynomial, which in this case is the second-degree (quadratic) polynomial given by

$$3Ax^2 + 2Bx + C$$

where A, B, and C are the coefficients from the original cubic polynomial. You then find the values of x for which this polynomial is zero.

For a quadratic polynomial given by

$$Ux^2 + Vx + W,$$

where $U, V,$ and W are any coefficients, the values of x for which the polynomial is zero are given by the well-known formulas

$$(-V + \sqrt{D}) / 2U \qquad \text{and} \qquad (-V - \sqrt{D}) / 2U$$

where D, the "discriminant", is given by

$$V^2 - 4UW.$$

Note that if D is negative, then there is no solution; if D is zero, there is only one solution, and if D is positive, there are two solutions. The values of x for which the derivative (quadratic) polynomial are zero are the values of x for which the original (cubic) are a local maximum or minimum. Note that there are zero, one, or two such values dpending on whether the discriminant is negative, zero, or positive. These values of x are then plugged back into the cubic to give the actual local maximum or minimum values of the polynomial.

Your program will perform the following steps: Prompt the user for the coefficients of the cubic polynomial; compute the coefficients of the derivative quadratic polynomial, and write out this polynomial, using an appropriate output format; compute the discriminant of the quadratic polynomial, and decide where there are zero, one, or two roots; compute the value(s) of the variable for which this polynomial is zero, and write out these values; finally, compute the values of the cubic polynomial at the values of the variable above, and write out these values.

CHAPTER 9

ARRAYS AND POINTERS

Needless to say, arrays are an important topic, and in C they are intimately connected with pointers. I like to start by pointing out that up to now we have studied "simple variables", where a variable holds only a single value, and that arrays are the first "structured variables", where one variable refers to a collection of several values. I think it helps to first show intuitively the concept of a one-dimensional list of values and the concept of indexing or subscripting, and only then show the actual C syntax for arrays.

- It is important to differentiate a pointer to an `int`, for example, and an array of `ints` -- even though the two have the same "type", they are different objects. In particular, declaring a pointer to an `int` doesn't actually create any `ints`, while declaring an array to `int` does. A blackboard diagram of the two helps to show the difference.

- Go over the meaning of an array identifier without subscripts; it is a pointer but a *constant* pointer -- you can't change the address of an array. Making matters even more complex is the fact that an array as a formal parameter *can* be changed -- remind students that "call by value" applies to arrays just like anything else, except that it is a pointer which is passed by value. The pointer can be modifed without modifying the actual array parameter.

- I spend a lot of time going over the correspondence between accessing arrays using pointers and accessing arrays using subscripts. I generally allow students to use whichever method they want in writing programs, but point out that the pointer method is more efficient. I do, however, require that students be able to read and understand code that processes arrays using pointers. (The test bank for this chapter covers both techniques.)

- Multi-dimensional arrays can be presented as a natural extension of one-dimensional arrays. Make sure students understand how multi-dimensional arrays are passed as parameters. I don't go into too much detail on using pointers with multi-dimensional arrays -- this can be quite confusing and not nearly as common in practice as using pointers with one-dimensional arrays.

TRANSPARENCY MASTERS

Declaration and a picture of an array
Example: filling, printing, summing array
Example: Counting each letter separately
Pointers and arrays
Four ways of summing an array
Arrays as function parameters
Bubblesort function
Effect of bubblesort on an array
A two-dimensional array
Example: printing and summing a two-dimensional array
Expressions equivalent to a[i][j]
Two-dimensional arrays and functions
Dynamic memory allocation of arrays

ANSWERS TO EXERCISES

1.   (a) lower bound -- The index of the first element of an array, or the smallest legal index. In C, the lower bound of an array is always 0.

        (b) subscript -- The index or integer expression which identifies a particular element of an array. The first element of an array has subscript 0, the second element subscript 1, etc.

        (c) out of bounds -- An index or subscript which is outside the range of legal values for a particular array, in other words less than zero or greater than the size of the array.

2.   int   a[SIZE] = {0, 2, 2, 3, 4};   Error: Too many initializers.
        int   b[SIZE - 5];   Error: Size is negative
        int   c[3.0]   Error: Size is floating (must be integer)

3.

```
void sum (double a[],
         int     n,
         double *even_index_sum_ptr,
         double *odd_index_sum_ptr)
{
    int    i;

    *even_index_sum_ptr = *odd_index_sum_ptr = 0;
    for (i = 0 ; i < n ; i ++)
       /* low-order bit of i is 1 if i is odd,
        * 0 if i is even
        */
       if (i & 1)
          *odd_index_sum_ptr += a[i];
       else
          *even_index_sum_ptr += a[i];
}
```

4.

```
void sum (int a[],
         int n,
         int *even_element_sum_ptr,
         int *odd_element_sum_ptr)
{
    int    i, el;

    *even_element_sum_ptr = *odd_element_sum_ptr = 0;
    for (i = 0 ; i < n ; i++)  {
       el = a[i];
       if (el & 1)
          *odd_element_sum_ptr += el;
       else
          *even_element_sum_ptr = el;
    }
}
```

5.

```c
/* Program to count each uppercase and lowercase
 * letter separately in an input file.  "u_letter"
 * and "l_letter" arrays hold the counts for each
 * uppercase and lowercase letter, respectively.
 */

#include <stdio.h>
#include <ctype.h>

main ()
{
    int    c, i, u_letter[26], l_letter[26];

    for (i = 0 ; i < 26 ; ++i)  {
        u_letter[i] = 0;
        l_letter[i] = 0;
    }

    while  ((c = getchar() ) != EOF)
        if (isupper(c))
            ++u_letter[c - 'A'];
        else if (islower(c))
            ++l_letter[c - 'a'];

    for (i = 0 ; i < 26 ; ++i)  {
        if (i % 6 == 0)
            putchar('\n');
        printf("%5c:%4d", 'A' + i, u_letter[i]);
    }

    putchar('\n');
    for (i = 0 ; i < 26 ; ++i)  {
        if (i % 6 == 0)
            putchar('\n');
        printf("%5c:%4d", 'a' + i, l_letter[i]);
    }
    printf("\n\n");
}
```

6. The first line of output is always 3 . The second line of output will be   6 on a 16-bit machine, and   12 on a 32-bit machine. The third line of output will be   12 on a machine where   sizeof(double) = 4 , and   24 on a machine with sizeof(double) = 8 . In the expression

```
(int *) p + 3,
```

the cast has higher precedence than the addition operator. In other words, p is cast as an integer before 3 is added. This means that p is incremented by the size of 3 integers, which is the same as the size of 6 chars if sizeof(int) = 2 or 12 chars if sizeof(int) = 4. In the expression

```
(char *) ( (int *) p + 3),
```

the pointer p is cast as an integer pointer, incremented by the size of 3 integers, and then cast back as a char pointer. In the expression

```
* (char *) ( (int *) p + 3),
```

the two unary operators associate right-to-left, so that the integer pointer is first cast as a char pointer, then dereferenced, to yield a char (not an int).

7. The following program uses bubble sort to sort an array of integers.

```
/* Program to sort an array of integers using bubble
 * sort.  The rand() function is used to initialize the
 * array to pseudo-random values.
 */

#include <stdio.h>

#define    SIZE 50

/* Exchange two integers.  Note the actual parameters
 * may be either addresses of simple integers or
 * addresses of elements in an integer array
 */
void swap (int *p1, int *p2)
{
    int    temp;

    temp = *p1;
    *p1 = *p2;
    *p2 = temp;
}
```

```c
/* Bubble sort an array of integers.
 * n is the size of a[]
 */
void bubble (int a[], int n)
{
    int     i, j;

    for (i = 0 ; i < n - 1 ; ++i)
       for (j = n - 1 ; i < j ; --j)
          if (a[j-1] > a[j])
             swap(&a[j-1], &a[j]);
}

/* Print an array of integers.  n is the size of a[] */
void print_array (int a[], int n)
{
    int     i;

    for (i = 0 ; i < n ; ++i)  {
       if (i % 6 == 0)
          putchar('\n');
       printf("%12d", a[i]);
    }
}

/* Fill an integer array with pseudo-random values.
 * n is the size of a[]
 */
void randomize (int a[], int n)
{
    int i;

    for (i = 0 ; i < n ; ++i)
       a[i] = rand();
}

main ()
{
    int     a[SIZE];

    randomize(a, SIZE);
    printf("Unsorted array of size %d:\n", SIZE);
    print_array(a, SIZE);

    bubble(a, SIZE);
    printf("\n\nSorted array:\n");
    print_array(a, SIZE);
    printf("\n\n");
}
```

The program below uses a version of bubblesort which terminates as soon as no two integers are interchanged in a pass. The second version is faster.

```
/* Program to sort an array of integers using bubble
 * sort.  The rand() function is used to initialize
 * the array to pseudo-random values.  The bubble
 * sort function is modified to terminate after a
 * pass in which no exchanges are made.
 */

#include <stdio.h>

#define   SIZE 50

/* Exchange two integers.  Note the actual parameters
 * may be either addresses of simple integers or
 * addresses of elements in an integer array
 */
void swap (int *p1, int *p2)
{
    int    temp;

    temp = *p1;
    *p1 = *p2;
    *p2 = temp;
}

/* Bubble sort an array of integers.  n is the size
 * of a[].  The sort terminates after a pass in which
 * no exchanges occur.  Changed is a boolean variable
 * which records whether an exhange occurred.
 */
void bubble (int a[], int n)
{
    int    i, j, Changed = 1;

    for (i = 0 ; (i < n - 1) && Changed ; ++i)   {
        Changed = 0;
        for (j = n - 1 ; i < j ; --j)
            if (a[j-1] > a[j])   {
                Changed = 1;
                swap(&a[j-1], &a[j]);
            }
    }
}
```

```
/* Print an array of integers.  n is the size of a[] */
void print_array (int a[], int n)
{
    int     i;

    for (i = 0 ; i < n ; ++i)  {
       if (i % 6 == 0)
          putchar('\n');
       printf("%12d", a[i]);
    }
}

/* Fill an integer array with pseudo-random values.
 * n is the size of a[]
 */
void randomize (int a[], int n)
{
   int i;

   for (i = 0 ; i < n ; ++i)
      a[i] = rand();
}

main ()
{
    int     a[SIZE];

    randomize(a, SIZE);
    printf("Unsorted array of size %d:\n", SIZE);
    print_array(a, SIZE);

    bubble(a, SIZE);
    printf("\n\nSorted array:\n");
    print_array(a, SIZE);
    printf("\n\n");
}
```

8. The program below finds the maximum and minimum elements of a two-dimensional array, without using functions.

```
/* Program to find maximum and minimum elements of
 * a two-dimensional array.  In this demonstration
 * program, no data is input to the array; since it
 * is an automatic array, it is initialized with
 * random values
 */

/* the definitions below imply a 5x4 array */
#define    ROWS 5
#define    COLS 4

#include <stdio.h>

main ()
{
    int     a[ROWS][COLS], row, col, el, min, max;

    min = a[0][0];
    max = min;
    for (row = 0 ; row < ROWS ; row++)
       for (col = 0 ; col < COLS ; col++)  {
           el = a[row][col];
           if (el > max)
              max = el;
           if (el < min)
              min = el;
       }

    printf("Minimum value is %d, and maximum is %d.\n",
                                        min, max);

}
```

9. The following program finds the maximum and mimimum values in a two-dimensional array using a function.

```c
/* Program to find maximum and minimum elements of a
 * two-dimensional array.  In this demonstration
 * program, no data is input to the array; since it is
 * an automatic array, it is initialized with random
 * values.
 */

/* the definitions below imply a 5x4 array */
#define   ROWS 5
#define   COLS 4

#include <stdio.h>

/* Find the minimum and maximum elements in a
 * two-dimensional array of ints.  COLS is the
 * number of columns, and n is the number of rows.
 */
void find_min_max (int a[][COLS], int n,
                   int *min_ptr, int *max_ptr)
{
    int    row, col, el;

    *min_ptr = a[0][0];
    *max_ptr = *min_ptr;
    for (row = 0 ; row < n ; row++)
       for (col = 0 ; col < COLS ; col++)   {
           el = a[row][col];
           if (el > *max_ptr)
              *max_ptr = el;
           if (el < *min_ptr)
              *min_ptr = el;
       }
}

main ()
{
    int    a[ROWS][COLS], row, col, el, min, max;

    find_min_max(a, ROWS, &min, &max);
    printf("Minimum value is %d, and maximum is %d.\n",
                                  min, max);
}
```

```
10.     /* Maintain sales data by month of highest sales.
         * Stores sales data by month for 10 years using a
         * two-dimensional array.  Rather than sort the entire
         * two-dimensional array, a second one-dimensional
         * array is filled with the toal sales for each month
         * over all 10 years, and this array is sorted. Another
         * one-dimensional array is initialized with the month
         * numbers 1 - 12.  Whenever the sort function
         * exchanges two numbers in the total sales array, the
         * corresponding entries in the month number array are
         * exchanged.  Thus month_number[1] will have the month
         * # of the highest sales, etc.
         */
        #include <stdio.h>

        #define    NYEARS    10

        int   sales_data [NYEARS] [12],
              sales_total [12],
              month_number [12] = {0,1,2,3,4,5,6,7,8,9,10,11};

        /* Read the initial sales data from standard input */
        void read_sales_data (int sales_data [] [12])
        {
              int   year, month;

              printf("\nReading sales data...\n");
              for (year = 0 ; year < NYEARS ; ++year)
                  for (month = 0 ; month < 12 ; ++month)
                      scanf("%d", &sales_data[year][month]);
        }

        /* compute total sales for each month */
        void compute_sales_total (int sales_data [][12],
                                  int sales_total[12])
        {
              int   year, month, tot;

              for (month = 0 ; month < 12 ; ++month) {
                  tot = 0;
                  for (year = 0 ; year < NYEARS ; ++year)
                      tot += sales_data[year][month];
                  sales_total[month] = tot;
              }
        }
```

(10. continued)

```c
/* swap two integers */
void swap (int *p1, int *p2)
{
      int   temp;

      temp = *p1;
      *p1 = *p2;
      *p2 = temp;
}


/* sort the total sales array in decending order.
 * at each exchange, the corresponding month_index
 * entries are also exchanged.
 */
void sort_sales_total (int data [],
                          int index [],
                 int n)
{
    int     i, j, Changed = 1;

    for (i = 0 ; (i < n - 1) && Changed ; ++i)   {
        Changed = 0;
        for (j = n - 1 ; i < j ; --j)
            if (data[j-1] < data[j])   {
                Changed = 1;
                swap(&data[j-1], &data[j]);
            swap(&index[j-1], &index[j]);
            }
    }
}
```

(10. continuned)

```
/* print the month name */
void print_month (int month)
{
     switch(month) {
     case 0:
          printf("Jan  "); break;
     case 1:
          printf("Feb  "); break;
     case 2:
          printf("Mar  "); break;
     case 3:
          printf("Apr  "); break;
     case 4:
          printf("May  "); break;
     case 5:
          printf("Jun  "); break;
     case 6:
          printf("Jul  "); break;
     case 7:
          printf("Aug  "); break;
     case 8:
          printf("Sep  "); break;
     case 9:
          printf("Oct  "); break;
     case 10:
          printf("Nov  "); break;
     case 11:
          printf("Dec  "); break;
     }
}
```

(10. continued)

```
/* print the sales data according to the order of
 * months given in the month_index array
 */
void print_sales_data (int sales_data [][12],
                       int month_index[])
{
     int  year, month, index, total;

     printf("Month    Yr 1  Yr 2  Yr 3  Yr 4   Yr 5");
     printf("Yr 6  Yr 7  Yr 8  Yr 9  Yr 10  Total\n");
     for (index = 0 ; index < 12 ; ++index) {
          month = month_index[index];
          print_month(month);
          total = 0;
          for (year = 0 ; year < NYEARS ; ++year) {
               printf("%6d", sales_data[year][month]);
               total += sales_data[year][month];
          }
          printf("%7d\n", total);
     }
}

main()
{
     read_sales_data(sales_data);
     compute_sales_total(sales_data, sales_total);
     printf("Original Sales Data (in $ millions):\n");
     print_sales_data(sales_data, month_number);
     sort_sales_total(sales_total, month_number, 12);
     printf("\n\nSales Data Sorted By Month:\n");
     print_sales_data(sales_data, month_number);
}
```

11. Here is another sorting algorithm:

```c
/* Program to demonstrate a simple transposition sort
 * on an aray of integers.  The array is printed after
 *  each pass.
 */
#define    SIZE 10

#include <stdio.h>

/* Exchange two integers.  Note the actual parameters
 * may be either addresses of simple integers or
 * addresses of elements in an integer array.
 */
void swap (int *p1, int *p2)
{
    int     temp;

    temp = *p1;
    *p1 = *p2;
    *p2 = temp;
}

/* Print an array of integers, n is the size of a[] */
void print_array (int a[], int n)
{
    int     i;

    for (i = 0 ; i < n ; ++i)   {
       if (i % 6 == 0)
          putchar('\n');
       printf("%10d", a[i]);
    }
}

/* Sort the array. It is printed after each pass. */
void trans_sort (int a[], int n)
{
    int     i, j;

    for (i = 0 ; i < n ; ++i)   {
       for (j = i + 1 ; j < n ; ++j)
          if (a[i] > a[j])
             swap(&a[i], &a[j]);

       printf("0fter pass %d:", i + 1);
       print_array(a, n);
    }
}
```

(11. continued)

```
/* Fill an integer array with pseudo-random values.
 * n is the size of a[]
 */
void randomize (int a[], int n)
{
    int i;

    for (i = 0 ; i < n ; ++i)
        a[i] = rand() % 100;
}

main ()
{
    int    a[SIZE];

    randomize(a, SIZE);
    printf("Unordered data:");
    print_array(a, SIZE);

    trans_sort(a, SIZE);
    printf("\n\n");
}
```

12. The program below is the same except each exchange is shown.

```
/* Program to demonstrate a simple transposition sort
 * on an array of integers.
 * The array is printed after each exchange.
 */
#define   SIZE 12

#include <stdio.h>

/* Exchange two integers. */
void swap (int *p1, int *p2)
{
    int    temp;

    temp = *p1;
    *p1 = *p2;
    *p2 = temp;
}
```

(12. continued)

```c
/* Print an array of integers.  n is the size of a[] */
void print_array (int a[], int n)
{
    int    i;

    for (i = 0 ; i < n ; ++i)
        printf("%4d", a[i]);
    putchar('\n');
}

/* Print out underscores underneath given array
 * positions
 */
void underscore_indicies (int i, int j)
{
    int    n;

    for (n = 0 ; n <= i || n <= j ; ++n)  {
        if (n == i || n == j)
            printf(" ---");
        else
            printf("    ");
    }
    putchar('0');
}

/* Sort the array.  It is printed after each exchange. */
void trans_sort (int a[], int n)
{
    int    i, j;

    for (i = 0 ; i < n ; ++i)
        for (j = i + 1 ; j < n ; ++j)
            if (a[i] > a[j])  {
                swap(&a[i], &a[j]);
                print_array(a, n);
                underscore_indicies(i, j);
            }
}

/* Fill an integer array with pseudo-random values. */
void randomize (int a[], int n)
{
    int i;

    for (i = 0 ; i < n ; ++i)
        a[i] = rand() % 100;
}
```

(12. continued)

```
main ()
{
    int      a[SIZE];

    randomize(a, SIZE);
    printf("Unordered data:");
    print_array(a, SIZE);

    trans_sort(a, SIZE);
    printf("\n\n");
}
```

13.
```
/* Program to count the number of occurrences of each
 * integer in input file.  The input is assumed to
 * contain 100 integers. The program first reads the
 * integers into an array, then uses bubble sort to
 * sort the array into descending order.  Occurrences
 * of the same integer will be next to each other in
 * the sorted array.
 */
#include <stdio.h>

#define    SIZE 100

/* Read integers into an array.
 * n is the size of the array.
 */
void read_array (int a[], int n)
{
    int      i;

    for (i = 0 ; i < n ; ++i)
        scanf("%d", &a[i]);
}

/* Swap two integers */
void swap (int *X, int*Y)
{
    int      Temp;

    Temp = *X;
    *X = *Y;
    *Y = Temp;
}
```

(13. continued)

```c
/* Bubble sort an array of integers. */
void bubble (int a[], int n)
{
    int    i, j, Changed = 1;

    for (i = 0 ; (i < n - 1) && Changed ; ++i)  {
        Changed = 0;
        for (j = n - 1 ; i < j ; --j)
            if (a[j-1] > a[j])  {
                Changed = 1;
                swap(&a[j-1], &a[j]);
            }
    }
}

/* Take a sorted array and print out how many times
 * each value occurs.
 */
void count_occurrences (int a[], int n)
{
    int    i = 0, Count, Value;

    /* loop for each distinct value in array */
    while (i < n)  {

        /* save value at current index */
        Value = a[i];
        Count = 1;

        /* loop as long as same value occurs in following
         * positions.  Note boolean condition depends on
         * partial evaluation and L-to-R ordering of &&
         */
        while (++i < n && a[i] == Value)
            ++Count;

        printf("%10d occurs %d times.\n", Value, Count);
        /* note index is left at first occurrence of next
         * value, or one past end of array
         */
    }
}
```

```
    main ()
    {
        int a[SIZE];

        printf("Reading %d integers...\n", SIZE);
        read_array(a, SIZE);

        bubble(a, SIZE);

        count_occurrences(a, SIZE);
    }
```

14. The program below is the same as the previous exercise except that `calloc`
is used to dynamically allocate the array.

```
/* Program to count the number of occurrences of each
 * integer in input file.  The first number in the input
 * is the number of integers following.  The program
 * first reads the integers into an array, then uses
 * bubble sort to sort the array into descending order.
 * Occurrences of the same integer will be next to each
 * other in the sorted array.
 */
#include <stdio.h>

/* Read integers into an array. */
void read_array (int a[], int n)
{
    int     i;

    for (i = 0 ; i < n ; ++i)
        scanf("%d", &a[i]);
}

void swap (int *X, int *Y)
{
    int     Temp;

    Temp = *X;
    *X = *Y;
    *Y = Temp;
}
```

```c
/* Bubble sort an array of integers.  n is the size
 * of a[]. The sort terminates after a pass in which
 * no exchanges occur.  Changed is a boolean variable
 * which records whether an exhange occurred.
 */
void bubble (int a[], int n)
{
    int    i, j, Changed = 1;

    for (i = 0 ; (i < n - 1) && Changed ; ++i)   {
        Changed = 0;
        for (j = n - 1 ; i < j ; --j)
            if (a[j-1] > a[j])   {
                Changed = 1;
                swap(&a[j-1], &a[j]);
            }
    }
}


/* Take a sorted array and print out how many times
 * each value occurs.
 */
void count_occurrences (int a[], int n)
{
    int    i = 0, Count, Value;

    /* loop for each distinct value in array */
    while (i < n)   {

        /* save value at current index */
        Value = a[i];
        Count = 1;

        /* loop as long as same value occurs in following
         * positions note boolean condition depends on
         * partial evaluation and L-to-R ordering of &&
         */
        while (++i < n && a[i] == Value)
            ++Count;

        printf("%10d occurs %d times.\n", Value, Count);
    }
}
```

```
main ()
{
    int *rand_array, size;

    /* read size of array, then allocate the array */
    scanf("%d", &size);
    rand_array = calloc(size, sizeof(int));
    read_array(rand_array, size);

    bubble(rand_array, size);

    count_occurrences(rand_array, size);
}
```

15. On our system, the output of the code is shown below. The two arrays are indeed different.

```
a[0] = 3     b[0] = 3
a[1] = 2     b[1] = 5
a[2] = 3     b[2] = 3
```

PROGRAMMING PROJECT 9-1

Purpose: One-dimensional arrays.

The simplest of all encryption methods is a *straight substitution* code, where one character is directly substituted for another. This is like the cryptograms found
in newspapers and puzzle books. For this assignment you are to write a pair of programs to do encoding and decoding using a code which just substitutes one letter for another. To keep things simple, all lower-case letters are converted to upper-case, and only letters are encoded; non-alphabetic characters (spaces, numbers, and punctuation marks) are left as they are. The *substitution key* consists of the twenty-six letters which substitute for the letters A through Z in order. A sample substitution key would be the following:

```
Letter:          ABCDEFGHIJKLMNOPQRSTUVWXYZ
Coded letter:    TFHXQJEMUPIDCKVBAOLRZWGNSY
```

```
Sample encoding:
Input line:    One if by land, two if by sea.
Encoded line: VKQ UJ FS DTKX, RGV UJ FS LQT.
```

The first program will encode plain text into encoded text. The first line of input will be the substitution key, exactly 26 letters on a line by itself. The first letter in the substitution key will be the code for 'A', the second character the code for 'B', and the twenty-sixth letter the code for 'Z'. Your program should check that no character is duplicated in the coding key, and that there are exactly 26 letters on the line. Following the substitution key will come the text to be encoded. The program reads the text character by character, translating and writing each alphabetic character according to the key, and writing the non-alphabetic characters unchanged. The substitution key should be stored in a one-dimensional array. The encoding is done by indexing the array using the character to be encoded.

The second program decodes encoded text into plain text. It reads in the substitution key on the first line of input in exactly the same format as the first program, but then uses the key to decode text that follows. It will be simpler to construct a decoding key in a separate one-dimensional array, rather than searching through the substitution key each time for the character.

PROGRAMMING PROJECT 9-2

Purpose: arrays, multi-dimensional arrays, simulation techniques

The goal of this exercise is to simulate the movement of an oil spill on the surface of a body of water. A number of simplifying assumptions need to be made in order for this to be practical. The surface of the water is divided into a two-dimensional grid of squares, represented by a two-dimensional array of numbers measuring the amount of oil in each square. Over time oil moves from one square into neighboring squares by diffusion and pushed by a prevailing wind. We will assume that the wind is always blowing from west to east (left to right on the display). The simulation proceeds in a series of discrete time steps, i.e. in a for-loop with an integer time step variable. At each time step, the following rules determine the movement of oil in the simulation:

E % of the oil in a square evaporates;

Of the remaining oil, $10 / (10 + V)$ of the oil remains in the same square, where V is the wind velocity in miles per hour;

Of the oil which does not evaporate and does not remain in the same square, 40% moves to the square immediately to the east, 20% moves into each of the squares to the north-east and the south-east; and 10% moves into each of the squares to the north and south.

Oil moving into squares beyond the bounds of the array is lost to the simulation. At each time step, the program goes through the entire array and calcualtes the amount of oil in each square based on the amounts in the neighboring squares at the previous time step. To do this correctly you need two arrays -- one to hold all the old values while the new values are computed, and one to hold the new values.

The state of the simulation at any time step is shown by displaying the contents of the array on the screen. To keep the display manageable, we assume that the maximum amount of oil in a square, measured in barrels, is 999, and only the digits to the left of the decimal point are displayed. Therefore each square in the grid takes up 3 digits plus a space in the display, and so the maximum array size that will fit on the screen is 20 columns by 23 rows. Since it would be impractical to generate this display at each time step, the program runs for a given number of time steps and then displays the array. Initially (at time step zero), a given amount of oil is spilled into the middle square in the westernmost column (middle of left edge of display), and all other squares are initialized to zero. The program inputs the following at the start of the run:

# of barrels spilled (between 0 and 999);
wind velocity in miles per hour (must be non-negative);
evaporation rate (fraction between zero and one);
# of time steps to run.

The program runs for the given number of steps and displays the resulting array. (There is no need to display the initial configuration.) It then inputs a number of time steps to run again, and again displays the result. In this way you can continue as long as desired. The end of the program is indicated by an end-of-file on input.

CHAPTER 10

STRINGS AND POINTERS

The topic of strings can be made less mysterious by starting from the observation that a string is just an array of characters. By this point, students should be becoming proficient in using arrays and pointers.

- The end of string sentinel, and the difference between the physical size of the array that holds the string, and the "logical" length of the string, which can change.

- Students should be exposed to common string processing techniques, in particular functions involving the `*p++` construction, such as is found in the string library.

You can have fun with this chapter. There are many interesting programming projects and class examples possible now that strings have been introduced.

TRANSPARENCY MASTERS

How a string is stored in an array
Example: Have a nice day
Strings and pointers
Processing a string using pointers
Example: Counting words
Arguments to `main()`
Standard library functions for string handling
Examples of library string functions

ANSWERS TO EXERCISES

1.

```c
/* "Nice_day" program using pointers instead of arrays
 */
#include <stdio.h>
#include <ctype.h>

#define   MAXSTRING 100

main ()
{
    char    *p, c, name [MAXSTRING];
    int     sum = 0;

    printf("\nHi! What is your name?   ");
    for (p = name ; (c = getchar()) != '\n' ; ++p)   {
        *p = c;
        if (isalpha(c))
            sum += c;
    }
    *p = '\0';
    printf("\n%s%s%s\n%s: ",
        "Nice to meet you ", name, ".",
        "Your name spelled backwards is");
    for (--p ; p >= name ; --p)
        putchar(*p);
    printf("\n%s%d%s\n\n%s\n",
        "and the letters in your name sum to ", sum, ".",
        "Have a nice day!");
}
```

2.
```
/* Word counting program using arrays instead of
 * pointers.  Lines exceeding MAXLINE characters
 * are broken up and counted separately.  With
 * MAXLINE = 80, words that wrap around the screen
 * will be counted as 2 separate words.
 */
#include <stdio.h>

#define    MAXLINE    80

int word_cnt (char s[])
{
    int cnt = 0, i = 0;

    while (s[i] != '\0')  {
        while (isspace(s[i]))
            ++i;
        if (s[i] != '\0')  {
            ++cnt;
            while (!isspace(s[i]) && s[i] != '\0')
                ++i;
        }
    }
    return cnt;
}

/* Function to read a line of input, terminated by
 * newline or exceeding array size. Returns 1 if a
 * line actually read, 0 if EOF encountered.
 * (Assumes unix convention that a newline always
 * precedes an EOF)
 */
int read_line (char s[], int length)
{
    int    c, i;

    for (i = 0 ; i < length-1 && (c = getchar()) != '\n'
                            && c != EOF ; ++i)
        s[i] = c;
    s[i] = '\0';
    return  (c != EOF);
}
```

(2. continued)

```
main ()
{
    char    s[MAXLINE];

    printf("Word counting program.\n");
    while (read_line(s, MAXLINE))
        printf("That line contained %d words.\n",
                word_cnt(s));
}
```

3. The following program reads strings, and scans each string for least and most frequently occurring characters.

```
#include <stdio.h>
#include <ctype.h>
#define     MAXSTRING 256

/* count occurrences of upper and lower case letters
 * in a string. If the string is empty, nulls will
 * be returned.
 */
void search (char *s, char *p_least, char *p_most,
             int *p_least_cnt, int *p_most_cnt)
{
    /* keep separate arrays for upper & lower case */
    int     uc_count[26], lc_count[26], i;

    /* initialize arrays to zeroes */
    for (i = 0 ; i < 26 ; ++i)
        uc_count[i] = lc_count[i] = 0;

    /* read the string char by char */
    while (*s != '\0') {
        if (isalpha(*s))
            if (isupper(*s))
                ++uc_count[*s - 'A'];
            else
                ++lc_count[*s - 'a'];
        ++s;
    }

    /* initialize the counters for min/max */
    *p_least = 0;
    *p_most = 0;
    *p_least_cnt = MAXSTRING;
    *p_most_cnt = 0;
```

(3. continued)

```
        /* check counts for min & max */
        for (i = 0 ; i < 26 ; ++i) {
        /* check lower-case counts */
        if (lc_count[i] > 0) {
            if (lc_count[i] < *p_least_cnt) {
                *p_least_cnt = lc_count[i];
                *p_least = i + 'a';
            }
            if (lc_count[i] > *p_most_cnt) {
                *p_most_cnt = lc_count[i];
                *p_most = i + 'a';
            }
        }
        /* check upper-case counts */
        if (uc_count[i] > 0) {
            if (uc_count[i] < *p_least_cnt) {
                *p_least_cnt = uc_count[i];
                *p_least = i + 'A';
            }
            if (uc_count[i] > *p_most_cnt) {
                *p_most_cnt = uc_count[i];
                *p_most = i + 'A';
            }
        }
    }
}

main ()
{
    char    str[MAXSTRING], least, most;
    int     least_cnt, most_cnt;

    for (;;) {
        printf("Enter a string to be scanned");
        printf(" (EOF to end): ");
        if (scanf("%s", str) == EOF)
            exit(0);
        search(str, &least, &most, &least_cnt, &most_cnt);
        printf("\nIn string '%s',\n", str);
        printf("Character %c occured least, ", least);
        printf("with %d occurrences.\n", least_cnt);
        printf("Character %c occured most, ", most);
        printf("with %d occurrences.\n", most_cnt);
    }
}
```

4.
```
/* Function to bubble sort the characters in a string */
void bubble_string (char *s)
{
      char *pi, *pj, *tail;

      /* point to last character */
      tail = s + strlen(s) - 1;
      for (pi = s ; pi < tail ; ++pi)
          for (pj = tail ; pi < pj ; --pj)
            if (*(pj - 1) > *pj)
                swap(pj - 1, pj);
}
```

5.
```
/* Program to echo command line arguments,
 * one per line.  If the -c option is present,
 * args following are printed with capital letters
 */
#include <stdio.h>

/* Print a string in uppercase letters, then newline */
void echo_upper (char *s)
{
    while (*s != '\0')  {
       putchar((islower(*s)) ? toupper(*s) : *s);
       ++s;
    }
    putchar('\n');
}

main (int argc, char *argv[])
{
    int    i, use_caps = 0;

    for (i = 1 ; i < argc ; ++i)
       if (!strcmp(argv[i], "-c"))
          use_caps = 1;
       else if (!use_caps)
          printf("%s\n", argv[i]);
       else
          echo_upper(argv[i]);
}
```

6. An implementation of the `strncmp` function follows. The function compares two strings lexicographically, but scans at most N characters.

```
/* Compare at most n characters lexicographically
 * in strings s1 and s2
 */
int strncmp (char *s1, char *s2, int n)
{
    if (n <= 0)     /* need a special case here */
        return 0;
    while (--n > 0 && *s1 == *s2 && *s1 != '\0')  {
        ++s1;
        ++s2;
    }
    return  *s1 - *s2;
}
```

7.

Expression	Equivalent expression	Value
`***p`	`p[0][0][0]`	`'a'`
`**p[1]`	`p[1][0][0]`	`'j'`
`**(p[1] + 2)`	`p[1][2][0]`	`'x'`
`*(*(p + 1) + 1)[7]`	`*((p[1] + 1)[7])`	*error*
`(*(*(p + 1) + 1))[7]`	`p[1][1][7]`	`'w'`
`*(p[1][2] + 2)`	`p[1][2][2]`	`'z'`

8. The output of the code is:

```
C. B. DeMogul is RICH RICH RICH!
C. B. DeMogul is poor poor poor!
```

The constant string `RICH!` is overwritten via the pointer `q`. The pointer `p` still points to the same memory area, but its value has been changed.

9. The program below will read in a number of strings and then sort them, using `strcmp` to determine order.

```c
/* Program to sort strings */
#include <stdio.h>
#include <string.h>

#define   N_STRINGS 7
#define STRING_MAX   256

/* Exchange two strings */
void swap (char *s1, char *s2)
{
    char    temp[STRING_MAX];

    strcpy(temp, s1);
    strcpy(s1, s2);
    strcpy(s2, temp);
}

/* Bubble sort an array of strings */
void bubble_strings (char s [] [STRING_MAX], int n)
{
    int     i, j;

    for (i = 0 ; i < n - 1 ; ++i)
        for (j = n - 1 ; i < j ; --j)
            if (strcmp(s[j-1], s[j]) > 0)
                swap(s[j - 1], s[j]);
}

main ()
{
    char    str [N_STRINGS] [STRING_MAX];
    int     i;

    printf("Enter %d strings:\n", N_STRINGS);
    for (i = 0 ; i < N_STRINGS ; ++i)
        scanf("%s", str[i]);

    bubble_strings(str, N_STRINGS);

    printf("The sorted list of strings is:\n");
    for (i = 0 ; i < N_STRINGS ; ++i)
        printf("%s\n", str[i]);
}
```

10. The following program will sort the command line arguments and print them. Since they are stored as an array of pointers, the sort is faster.

```c
/* Program to print command line arguments in
 * lexographic sorted order.  Since they are stored
 * as an array of pointers, sorting is faster since
 * only pointers need to be swapped.
 */ #include <stdio.h> #include <string.h>

/* Exchange two string pointers */ void swap (char
**s1, char **s2) {
   char    *temp;

   temp = *s1;
   *s1 = *s2;
   *s2 = temp; }

/* Bubble sort an array of string pointers */ void
bubble_strings (char **s, int n) {
   int     i, j;

   for (i = 0 ; i < n - 1 ; ++i)
      for (j = n - 1 ; i < j ; --j)
         if (strcmp(s[j-1], s[j]) > 0)
            swap(&s[j-1], &s[j]); }

main (int argc, char **argv) {
   int     i;

   bubble_strings(argv, argc);

   printf("The sorted list of command line arguments
is:\n");
   for (i = 0 ; i < argc ; ++i)
      printf("%s\n", argv[i]); }
```

PROGRAMMING PROJECT 10-1

Purpose: string processing

Write a program to read text from standard input and echo it to standard output, but with all palindromes converted to upper case. A palindrome is a word which is the same backwards as forwards, for example "civic" or "radar". A word is defined to be any sequence of upper or lower case letters, but not numbers, punctuation, or blank space. You may assume that words are not hyphenated or otherwise carried across line boundaries. The end of the input will be end-of-file. For this problem there is no minimum word size for palindromes, so that for example all single letter words would be considered palindromes. The program should not change the input in any way other than capitalizing palindromes. The program should be case sensitive, so that "Civic" would NOT be a palindrome.

A sample run, with use input in boldface, is shown below:

This is a test of the new civic radar.

This is a test of the new CIVIC RADAR.

PROGRAMMING PROJECT 10-2

Purpose: string processing.

Write a program to translate input text into pig latin. The translation is done word-by-word. The program should read each word of input, and check the first character of the word. If the first character is a vowel ('a', 'e', 'i', 'o', or 'u'), it writes out the word with 'bay' added at the end. If the first character of the word is not a vowel, it writes out the word without its first character, and adds the original first character of the word plus 'ay' at the end. Any blanks and punctuation marks should not be counted as part of a word, but should be written just as they are read. The program continues until an end of file is read. A sample run, with input in boldface, is shown below:

```
Language translator program; enter lines of text:
```
pray to heaven, but row to shore!

```
raypay otay eavenhay, utbay owray otay horesay!
```

<cntrl-d>

Your program should use the following two functions:

ReadWord -- takes a single parameter of type pointer to string. It skips any blanks or other non-alphabetic characters, reads a word, and returns the word in the string parameter. Note this function must also print any non-alphabetic characters which it skips.

TranslateWord -- takes a single parameter of type pointer to string. The string will contain the word read by ReadWord. It tests the first character of the word and writes out the appropriate translation.

CHAPTER 11

THE PREPROCESSOR AND SOFTWARE METHODOLOGY

C is unique in its reliance on the preprocessor; in many languages, the programmer is not necessarily aware that a preprocessor exists. Up until now the text has briefly mentioned the existence of the preprocessor and hinted at some of its functions. Now it is covered in detail. This chapter could be skipped if time is short, or just skimmed over in one class period. The important points in the chapter are:

● Students should be made aware of the difference between what happens at "compile-time" and what happens at "run-time", and that the preprocessor only works at the former.

● Macros with arguments can be covered in more or less detail, according to class needs. The student should be made aware that macros can be prone to subtle errors, and can make the code less clear. Excessive use of macros should be avoided. Several of the short answer testbank questions illustrate various kinds of errors which can occur with macros.

● Developing a large program in separately compiled modules is useful practical knowledge, along with the use of `#include`-d header files to coordinate them.

TRANSPARENCY MASTERS

The `#include` directive
The `#define` directive with no arguments
A simple macro with arguments
The `qsort()` function
Outline of a program using `qsort`
Conditional compilation
The "stringization" operator
Example header file for a large program (*mk_cols*)
Common mistakes using macros

ANSWERS TO EXERCISES

2. The program below illustrates the definition and use of an exclusive-or macro. All combinations of boolean values are tested.

```
/* Generate and test an XOR macro */

#define   XOR(x,y)   (!(x) && (y) || (x) && !(y))

main ()
{
   int    a,b;

   printf("%5s%5s%5s\n--------------\n",
          "x", "y", "XOR");
   for (a = 0 ; a <= 1 ; a++)
      for (b = 0 ; b <= 1 ; b++)
         printf("%5d%5d%5d\n", a, b, XOR(a,b));
}
```

3. The program below illustrates the definition and use of 3-parameter and 4-parameter exclusive or macros. All possible combinations of boolean values are tested. (NOTE: The definitions in the exercise are different from a more common definition of exclusive or, which is that an odd number of the arguments are true.)

```
/* Generate and test XOR_3 and XOR_4 macros */

/* The definitions below use the ! operator to force
 * the value to be either 0 or 1; then the boolean
 * values can be simply added together.  This is
 * simpler & faster than the full boolean expression.
 */
#define XOR_3(x,y,z)    (!(x) + !(y) + !(z) == 2)
#define XOR_4(x,y,z,w)  (!(x) + !(y) + !(z) + !(w) == 3)

/* Generate truth tables for the exclusive-or macros */
main ()
{
    int     a, b, c, d;

    printf("%5s%5s%5s%8s\n------------------------\n",
                        "x", "y", "z", "XOR_3");
    for (a = 0 ; a <= 1 ; a++)
       for (b = 0 ; b <= 1 ; b++)
          for (c = 0 ; c <= 1 ; c++)
             printf("%5d%5d%5d%8d\n",
                    a, b, c, XOR_3(a, b, c));

    printf("\n%5s%5s%5s%5s%8s\n",
                        "x", "y", "z", "w", "XOR_4");
    printf("--------------------------\n");
    for (a = 0 ; a <= 1 ; a++)
       for (b = 0 ; b <= 1 ; b++)
          for (c = 0 ; c <= 1 ; c++)
             for (d = 0 ; d <= 1 ; d++)
                printf("%5d%5d%5d%5d%8d\n", a, b, c, d,
                                XOR_4(a, b, c, d));
}
```

4. No, it is not possible to `#define` XOR as a binary operator. In order to be called as a XOR b , XOR would have to be defined as a macro with no arguments.

```
5.    /* Generate and test PRN_STRING macro */
      #include <stdio.h>

      #define   PRN_STRING(x)   printf("%s %d\n", x, strlen(x));

      main ()
      {
         char    s[256];

         printf("Enter strings, EOF to end:\n");
         while (scanf("%s", s) != EOF)
            PRN_STRING(s)
      }
```

8. The program below illustrates the definition and use of a macro using the stringization operator to print the names and values of 3 variables.

```
      /* Generate and test a PRN3 macro */
      #include <stdio.h>

      #define   PRN3(x,y,z)      printf(#x " has value %g\n"\
                     #y " has value %g\n"\
                     #z " has value %g\n", x, y, z)

      main ()
      {
         float     A, B, C;

         printf("Enter floating values for A, B, and C:\n");
         scanf("%f%f%f", &A, &B, &C);
         PRN3(A, B, C);
      }
```

9. Here is a definition for a 3-place "max" macro:

```
      #define    max(x, y, z)     (((x) > (y)) ?\
                              ( (x) > (z) ? (x) : (z) )\
                     ( (y) > (z) ? (y) : (z) ) )
```

Since the arguments appear more than once in the definition, any invocation of the macro involving side-effects will produce unexpected results, e.g.:

```
      int  A[100], *pa = A;

      /* find the maximum of the first three elements */
         /* or so the programmer thinks */
      biggest = max(pa++, pa++, pa++);   /* wrong */
```

11. The output is the following:

```
value of a[0]:  2
value of a[1]:  3
value of a[2]:  5
value of a[3]:  7
value of a[4]:  11
value of a[5]:  13
value of a[6]:  17
value of a[7]:  19
```

The output will be the same with the alternate `printf` statement; you can either print the three strings using three `%s`'s, or concatenate them into one string and print it using a single `%s`.

13. Here is a program using a macro to fill an array:

```
#include <stdio.h>

#define       FILL(array, size)      \
              for (i = 0; i < size; ++i)      \
                  array[i] = rand() % 100

#define       ARY_SIZE   20

main ()
{
     int   i, A[ARY_SIZE];

     FILL(A, ARY_SIZE);

     printf("Contents of randomly filled array: \n");
     for (i = 0 ; i < ARY_SIZE ; ++i) {
         if (i % 6 == 0)
             putchar('\n');
         printf("%12d", A[i]);
     }
     putchar('\n');
}
```

14. The program using the `FILL` macro with a local variable will not compile in the example shown because the macro invocation is followed by a semicolon, but the macro body is enclosed in braces, and a semicolon which follows a right brace will end the if-statement.

16. One reason the name of the program is not hard-wired into the code is to allow it to present an appropriate example (when the -h option is used) if the executable file is renamed. If the -4 and -u options are interchanged on the command line, the program will run exactly the same.

17. To add the -1 option, the get_options() and mk_cols() functions are modified as follows. The prn_info() function might also be modified to add help about the 1 option. The *mk_cols.h* file should also be modified to change the enumeration type.

```c
#include "mk_cols.h"

static void      capitalize (char *w);
static void      uncapitalize (char *w);

static char    * get_word (char *w);

void mk_cols(int n_cols, lu_option cnvrt)
{
    char    w[MAXWORD];
    int     col_cnt, col_width, i, n_blanks;

    col_cnt = n_blanks = 0;
    col_width = SCREEN_WIDTH / n_cols;
    while (get_word(w) != NULL)  {
        switch (cnvrt)  {
            case none:
                break;
            case upper:
                capitalize(w);
                break;
            case lower:
                uncapitalize(w);
                break;
        }
        for (i = 0 ; i < n_blanks ; ++i)
            putchar(' ');
        printf("%s", w);
        if (++col_cnt >= n_cols)  {
            putchar('\n');
            col_cnt = n_blanks = 0;
        }
        else
            n_blanks = col_width - strlen(w);
    }
    if (col_cnt != 0)
        putchar('\n');
}
```

```c
void get_options (int argc, char **argv,
              int *n_cols_ptr, lu_option *case_ptr)
{
    char    *pgm_name = argv[0];
    int     i, n_cols = N_COLS;
    lu_option   cnvrt = none;

    for (i = 1 ; i < argc ; ++i)  {
        if (*argv[i] != '-')   {
            printf("ERROR: Inappropriate argument.\n");
            prn_info_pgm_name);
            exit(1);
        }
        if (strcmp(argv[i], "-h") == 0)   {
            prn_info(pgm_name);
            exit(1);
        }
        if (isdigit(argv[i][1]))
            sscanf(argv[i] + 1, "%d", &n_cols);
        else if (strcmp(argv[i], "-u") == 0)   {
            if (cnvrt == lower)   {
                printf("ERROR: Can't have both -l and -u.\n");
                exit(1);
            }
            else
                cnvrt = upper;
        }
        else if (strcmp(argv[i], "-l") == 0)   {
            if (cnvrt == upper)   {
                printf("ERROR: Can't have both -l and -u.\n");
                exit(1);
            }
            else
                cnvrt = lower;
        }
        else  {
            printf("ERROR: Unknown option.\n");
            prn_info(pgm_name);
            exit(1);
        }
    }
    *n_cols_ptr = n_cols;
    *case_ptr = cnvrt;
}
```

```
static void capitalize (char *w)
{
    for ( ; *w != '\0' ; ++w)
        if (islower(*w))
            *w = toupper(*w);
}

static void uncapitalize (char *w)
{
    for ( ; *w != '\0' ; ++w)
        if (isupper(*w))
            *w = tolower(*w);
}

static char *get_word (char *w)
{
    char *p = w;
    int     c;

    while (isspace (c = getchar() ))
        ;
    if (c == EOF)
        return NULL;
    *p++ = c;
    while (!isspace (c = getchar()) && c != EOF)
        *p++ = c;
    *p = '\0';
    return w;
}
```

18. To redefine a word to contain only alphabetic characters, and to skip all other characters, only the "get_word()" function needs to be modified:

```
static char *get_word (char *w)
{
    char *p = w;
    int    c;

    /* skip anything other than alpha chars */
    while (! isalpha (c = getchar() ))
        ;
    if (c == EOF)
        return NULL;
    *p++ = c;

    /* collect characters as long as they are alpha*/
    while (isalpha (c = getchar()) && c != EOF)
        *p++ = c;
    *p = '\0';
    return w;
}
```

19. To add the ability to read numbers instead of words, a new no_yes variable numeric is added which records whether the -n option was used. File *main.c* is modified as follows:

```
#include "mk_cols.h"

main (int argc, char **argv)
{
    int         n_cols;
    no_yes u_case, numeric;

    get_options(argc, argv, &n_cols, &u_case, &numeric);
    mk_cols(n_cols, u_case, numeric);
}
```

The main change is the addition of a `get_number` function in the file *mk_cols.c*:

```
/* Get a number from the input file, in character form.
 * Accepts a leading minus sign and embedded decimal,
 * but does not interpret exponential notation.
 * Must have digit before decimal, e.g. 0.5 not .5.
 */
static char *get_number (char *w)
{
    char *p = w;
    int  c, last_c = 0;

    /* skip up to next digit or EOF */
    while (!isdigit(c = getchar()) && c != EOF)
     last_c = c; /* save last char to check for minus */

    if (c == EOF)
        return(NULL);

    /* output minus if present */
    if (last_c == '-')
        *p++ = '-';

    /* read digits before decimal */
    while (isdigit(c)) {
        *p++ = c;
         c = getchar();
    }

    /* check for decimal, read remainder of # if present */
    if (c == '.') {
        *p++ = '.';
        while (isdigit(c = getchar()))
            *p++ = c;
    }
    *p = '\0';
    return w;
}
```

The condition of the while-loop in `mk_cols()` is changed to call `get_number()` instead of `get_word` if the numeric option is present:

```
while (((numeric == yes)
                ? get_number(w)
                    : get_word(w)) != NULL)...
```

The function `get_options()` is modifed to check for the new option:

```c
#include "mk_cols.h"

void get_options (int argc, char **argv,
                  int *n_cols_ptr,
                  no_yes *u_case_ptr,
                  no_yes *numeric_ptr)
{
    char        *pgm_name = argv[0];
    int         i, n_cols = N_COLS;
    no_yes u_case = no, numeric = no;

    for (i = 1 ; i < argc ; ++i)  {
        if (*argv[i] != '-')  {
            printf("ERROR: Inappropriate argument.\n");
            prn_info(pgm_name);
            exit(1);
        }
        if (strcmp(argv[i], "-h") == 0)  {
            prn_info(pgm_name);
            exit(1);
        }
        if (isdigit(argv[i][1]))
            sscanf(argv[i] + 1, "%d", &n_cols);
        else if (strcmp(argv[i], "-u") == 0)
            u_case = yes;
        else if (strcmp(argv[i], "-n") == 0)
            numeric = yes;
        else  {
            printf("ERROR: Unknown option.\n");
            prn_info(pgm_name);
            exit(1);
        }
    }
    *n_cols_ptr = n_cols;
    *u_case_ptr = u_case;
    *numeric_ptr = numeric;
}
```

20. To add the ability to change the flag character, the function "get_options()" is modified as follows. Also, the "prn_info()" function is rewritten to display the appropriate flag character when help is displayed.

```c
void get_options (int argc, char **argv,
                  int *n_cols_ptr, no_yes *u_case_ptr)
{
    char    *pgm_name = argv[0];
    int     i, n_cols = N_COLS;
    no_yes u_case = no;

    for (i = 1 ; i < argc ; ++i)   {
        if (*argv[i] != FLAG)   {
            printf("ERROR: Inappropriate argument.\n");
            prn_info(pgm_name);
            exit(1);
        }
        if (strcmp(argv[i]+1, "h") == 0)   {
            prn_info(pgm_name);
            exit(1);
        }
        if (isdigit(argv[i][1]))
            sscanf(argv[i] + 1, "%d", &n_cols);
        else if (strcmp(argv[i]+1, "u") == 0)
            u_case = yes;
        else   {
            printf("ERROR: Unknown option.\n");
            prn_info(pgm_name);
            exit(1);
        }
    }
    *n_cols_ptr = n_cols;
    *u_case_ptr = u_case;
}
```

(20. continued)

```
void prn_info (char *pgm_name)
{
    printf("\nUsage:      %s  [%ch] [%cN] [%cu]\n\n",
                    pgm_name, FLAG, FLAG, FLAG);
    printf("Example:    %s  %c7  < input  > output\n\n",
                    pgm_name, FLAG);
    printf("Words from the standard input file are");
    printf(" printed in N columns.\n\n");
    printf("Options:\n");
    printf("    %ch  help option, print this message\n",
                    FLAG);
    printf("    %cN  number of columns, by default %d\n",
                    FLAG, N_COLS);
    printf("    %cu  uppercase option\n", FLAG);
}
```

21. The tokens "Alice", "Bob", and "Carole" do not have to be declared because they are not variables; they are arguments to the macro. The preprocessor creates strings out of them since their occurrence in the macro "greetings" is preceded by the stringization operator.

22. The `compare_fractional_part` function is modified below to compare the entire numbers if the fractional parts are equal.

```
int compare_fractional_part (const void *vp,
                             const void *vq)
{
    const float    *p = vp, *q = vq;
    float      fract_diff, all_diff;

    p_fract = fractional_part(*p);
    q_fract = fractional_part(*q);
    fract_diff = fractional_part(*p) -
                     fractional_part(*q);
    all_diff = *p - *q;

    return (fract_diff < 0.0) ? -1 :
           (fract_diff > 0.0) ? 1 :
           (all_diff < 0.0) ? -1 :
              (all_diff > 0.0) ? 1 : 0;
}
```

23. The new `lexico` function is equivalent to the old version because it is merely casting the `void *` pointers to `char *` pointers before dereferencing, instead of assigning them to separate `char *` pointers -- what are being dereferenced and compared in either case are syntactically pointers to characters.

24. The reason for the construct

```
#ifndef    MK_COLS_H
#define    MK_COLS_H
...
#endif
```

is to guard against duplicate definitions. When all the source files are concatenated into one, there are three `#include`s of the header file. The first will define the symbol `MK_COLS_H`, causing the latter two to discover that `MK_COLS_H` is already defined, and they will skip the header definitions.

CHAPTER 12

RECURSION

This is a "conceptual" chapter. No new programming constructs are introduced; students have in principle been able to program recursive functions since chapter 4. The only feature of the language that needs to be addressed at this point is the fact that when a function calls itself, there is a separate copy of the parameters and local variables for each call. Other than that, lecture time is best devoted to the behavoir of recursive algorithms. Many students will be surprised by the behavoir of even simple recursive functions.

I find that a asking lot of "what is the output of the following recursive function..." type of question is useful. In particular, I have found that students who have never been exposed to recursion are prone to get the return from a recursive call wrong -- they forget that it returns to itself as many times as it called itself.

Students will find it easier to write recursive functions if they are reminded to first re-state the problem recursively.

Many of the examples in the text will seem somewhat artificial, and could be better done using iteration (with the significant exception of the *minmax* program). Many "real" applications of recursion, such as trees and other recursive data structures, don't appear until the student has advanced further into computer science. This chapter could conceivably be skipped in a course for non-computer science majors, most of whom will probably never use recursion, although of course computer science majors will eventually have to become expert with it.

TRANSPARENCY MASTERS

Blast off! (recursively)
Recursive sum program and call trace
Recursive string handling
Recursive string length
The best possible mixmax algorithm
Recursion errors: Forgetting the base case
Recursion errors: Incomplete base case test
Recursion errors: Decrement operator

ANSWERS TO EXERCISES

1. The initial call to `count_down()` causes the if-statement to be executed (not the "else"). However, the recursive call to `count_down()` occurs before the `printf("%d !   ", n)`. This means that the entire sequence of recursive calls and returns will occur before any exclamation points are printed. `BLAST OFF` is printed when `count_down()` is called with a zero argument, and only then do the recursive calls return to the `printf("%d !   ", n)`.

2. Here is a recursive progam to check for palindromes:

```
/* Recursive implementation of palindrome checker */

#include <stdio.h>
#define   STRINGMAX 256

/* Recursive function to check for palindrome
 * Takes as parameters pointers to first and last
 * character in string.  Recursive calls return
 * with value 1 when the two pointers meet or cross
 * (all characters in string checked), and return
 * with value 0 when the characters pointed to are
 * different.
 */
int ispalindrome (char *head, char *tail)
{
    return ( (head >= tail) || (*head == *tail) &&
                    ispalindrome(++head, --tail) );
}

/* the main program sets up the pointer to the tail
 * of the string and initiates the recusive call.
 */
main ()
{
    char   S [STRINGMAX];

    for     (;;)   {
        printf("Enter a string:   ");
        if (scanf("%s", S)  != 1)
            break;
        printf("\n%s is ", S);
        if (! ispalindrome(S, S + strlen(S) - 1))
            printf("not ");
        printf("a palindrome.\n");
    }
}
```

Here is an iterative version of the program:

```
/* Iterative version of palindrome checker */
#include <stdio.h>
#include <string.h>

#define   STRINGMAX 256

/* return 1 if a string is a palindrome, 0 otherwise */
int ispalindrome (char *Head)
{
    char   *Tail;

    for (Tail = Head + strlen(Head) - 1 ;
        Head < Tail && *Head == *Tail ;
      ++Head,  --Tail)
          ;
    return Head >= Tail;
}

main ()
{
    char   S [STRINGMAX];
    for (;;)   {
        printf("Enter a string:   ");
        if (scanf("%s", S) != 1)
          break;
        printf("\n%s is ", S);
        if (!ispalindrome(S))
          printf("not ");
        printf("a palindrome.\n");
    }
}
```

3. In the second return statement, `return (n + sum(--n))`, some compilers will evaluate the left side of the `+` before the right side, i.e. before `n` is decremented, and some compilers will evaluate the left side after the right side, i.e. after `n` is decremented, yielding an incorrect result. This is an example of the danger of using expressions with side-effects.

4. The base case given in the exercise will also work, but is slightly less efficient. The difference between the two is the `*s2 == 0` check. But the first part of the if-expression is `*s1 != *s2`; therefore the rest of the if-expression will only be checked if this is false, i.e. if `*s1 == *s2`, and so it is not necessary to check both `*s1 == 0` and `*s2 == 0`.

5. A recursive version of `strcmp` is given below.

```
/* Recursive string comparison and test program */
#include <string.h>
#include <stdio.h>

#define   MAXWORD   30   /* max characters in a word */
#define   N      50    /* number of words in the array */

int r_strcmp(char *s1, char *s2)
{
    if (*s1 != *s2 || *s1 == '\0')
        return(*s1 - *s2);
    else
        return(r_strcmp(++s1, ++s2));
}

main ()
{
    int    i, j;
    char   word [N] [MAXWORD], /* an array of N words */
      temp[MAXWORD];

    for (i = 0 ; i < N ; ++i)
        scanf("%s", word[i]);

    for (i = 0 ; i < N - 1 ; ++i)
        for (j = i + 1 ; j < N ; ++j)
            if (r_strcmp(word[i], word[j]) > 0)   {
                strcpy(temp, word[i]);
                strcpy(word[i], word[j]);
                strcpy(word[j], temp);
            }

    for (i = 0 ; i < N ; ++i)
        printf("%s\n", word[i]);
}
```

6. A recursive version of `strcpy` is given below. The function copies its second argument into its first argument.

```
char *    r_strcpy(char *s1, char *s2)
{
    if (*s1 = *s2)    /* copy char and test for null */
        r_strcpy(s1 + 1, s2 + 1);
    return(s1);
}
```

7. The second `printf` will cause difficulty, since the destination string is shorter than the source string. The `strcpy` function does not check for this, so whatever happens to follow the constant string and in memory will be overwritten. We can rewrite `strcpy` to check for a null character in the destination string. (However this will cause difficulty if the destination string is other than a constant string, since there will not necessarily be a null character anywhere in the destination). Notice that a static variable is not used, as was suggested.

```
char *    r_strcpy(char *s1, char *s2)
{
    /* check for overwriting a null */
    if (*s1 == '\0') {
      printf("ERROR: r_strcpy overwrote null.\n");
      exit(1);
    }
    if (*s1 = *s2)    /* copy char and test for null */
      r_strcpy(s1 + 1, s2 + 1);
    return(s1);
}
```

8.
```
/* Program to demonstrate co-recursive functions
 * One function counts the alphabetic characters in
 * a string, and the other sums the digits in the
 * same string. The functions use "call by reference"
 * so that both values can be passed to recursive
 * calls and returned to the main program.  This is
 * less efficient than static variables, but allows the
 * values to be returned to "main" in a cleaner way.
 */

/* prototype needed for mutual recursion */
void sum_digit (char *, int *, int *);

void count_alph (char *S, int *alpha_count,
                         int *digit_sum)
{
    if (*S)  {
      if (isalpha(*S))
        ++ (*alpha_count);
      sum_digit(S, alpha_count, digit_sum);
    }
}
```

```
void sum_digit (char *S, int *alpha_count,
                          int *digit_sum)
{
   if (isdigit(*S))
      (*digit_sum) += (*S - '0');
   count_alph(++S, alpha_count, digit_sum);
}

/* Here is an iterative version */
void count_and_sum (char *S, int *alpha_count,
                             int *digit_sum)
{
   *alpha_count = *digit_sum = 0;

   while (*S)  {
      if (isalpha(*S))
         ++ (*alpha_count);
      else if (isdigit(*S))
         (*digit_sum) += *S - '0';
      ++S;
   }
}

/* main function to test both versions
 * Note that the call-by-reference arguments must
 * be initialized to zero outside the recursive
 * function, but are initialized inside the
 * iterative version.
 */
main ()
{
   int    alpha_count = 0, digit_sum = 0;
   char   String [256];

   printf("Enter a string:  ");
   scanf("%256s", String);

   count_alph(String, &alpha_count, &digit_sum);
   printf("According to co-recursive functions:\n");
   printf("The string contains %d letters,", alpha_count);
   printf(" and the digits sum to %d.\n", digit_sum);

   count_and_sum(String, &alpha_count, &digit_sum);
   printf("According to iterative function:\n");
   printf("The string contains %d letters,", alpha_count);
   printf("and the digits sum to %d.\n", digit_sum);
}
```

```
9.      /* Program to demonstrate recursive and iterative
         *   functions for finding greatest common denominator
         */
        #include <stdio.h>

        /* Recursive version */
        int gcd (int a, int b)
        {
            int     r;

            if ((r = a % b) == 0)
                return b;
            else
                return gcd(b, r);
        }


        /* Equivalent iterative version */
        int iter_gcd (int a, int b)
        {
            int     r;

            while ((r = a % b) != 0)  {
                a = b ;
                b = r;
            }
            return b;
        }

        main ()
        {
            int     a, b;

            printf("Enter two integers: ");
            scanf("%d%d", &a, &b);

            printf("According to recursive function,");
            printf("the gcd is %d.\n", gcd(a,b));
            printf("According to iterative function,");
            printf("the gcd is %d.\n", iter_gcd(a, b));
        }
```

```
10.    /* Program to demonstrate recursive binary search */
       #include <stdio.h>

       #define   SIZE 50

       /* Fill an array of size n with random integers */
       void fill (int *a, int n)
       {
           int    i;

           for (i = 0 ; i < n ; ++i)
               a[i] = random() % 100;
       }

       /* binary search a sorted array of size n
        * returns address of entry containing value v
        * (does not return index because recursive
        * calls have don't have original array base)
        * or 0 if not found
        */
       int *look_up (int v, int *a, int n)
       {
           int    mid = n / 2;

           /* not found if we are down to size 0 */
           if (n <= 0)
               return(0);
           /* check for value in midpoint of given array */
           if (v == a[mid])
               return(a + mid);
           /* if not there search either half of array
            * depending on value
            */
           if (v > a[mid])
               return(look_up(v, a + mid + 1, n - mid - 1));
           else
               return(look_up(v, a, mid));
       }
```

(10. continued)

```
main ()
{
    int    a [SIZE], *found, i, v;
    void   bubble_sort(int [], int);

    fill(a, SIZE);
    bubble_sort(a, SIZE);
    printf("Sorted array of size %d:\n", SIZE);
    for (i = 0 ; i < SIZE ; ++i)
       printf("%3d", a[i]);

    printf("\nEnter value to search for: ");
    scanf("%d", &v);
    found = look_up(v, a, SIZE);
    if (found == 0)
       printf("Value not found in array.\n");
    else
       printf("Value found at index %d.\n", found - a);
}
```

11. The iterative algorithm for the min-max problem requires $2 \cdot (N - 1)$ comparisons, one each for the minimum and maximum for each element in the array after the first, which is used as the initializer for both min and max. The recursive algorithm reduces this by using the same comparison between two elements in the base case as a step in computing both the minimum and maximum. If $N = 2$, one comparison is required. If $N = 4$, then there are two bases cases, each with one comparison, and one recursive call, with two comparisons, for a total of 4 comparisons. In general, if N is a power of 2, there will be $N / 2$ base cases, each with one comparison, and $N / 2 - 1$ recursive calls, each with two comparisons, for a total of $N + N / 2 - 2$ comparisons.

12. The original `minmax` algorithm cannot be modified so that its base case is n equal to 1 instead of 2, and still remain optimal. The important feature of the original algorithm is that with a base case of two elements, a single comparison determines both the minimum and maximum of the two.

The reason the modified algorithm uses `n - n/2` where the original algorithm used `n/2` is to make sure the entire array is covered if the array size is not a power of 2. If the array size is not a power of two, then truncation will occur at some point when using `n/2` as the length of the right half of the list. The correct formula for the size of the right sublist is the total list size minus the size used for the left sublist in the recursive call, r `n - n/2`.

13.
```
/* Compute and print the connectivity of an (empty)
 * chessboard as viewed by a knight, which is the number
 * of legal moves the knight can make from each square.
 * Note this program is not recursive, but it is used in
 * the * recursive problems that follow.
 * It's not necessary to excplicitly represent the
 * chessboard as an array for this problem, but we do
 * so it can be used ith the Knight's Tour problem.
 */
#include <stdio.h>
#define    HEIGHT      8
#define    WIDTH       8

/* Check to see if a given (X, Y) coodinate is on the
 * board (0..7, 0..7)
 */
int on_board (int X, int Y)
{
     return X >= 0 && X < WIDTH && Y >= 0 && Y < HEIGHT;
}


/* Check the connectivity for a given square
 * Note the knight can move
 *    +/- 1 horizontally and +/1 2 vertically,
 *    or +/- 2 horizontailly and +/- vertically.
 */
int Connectivity (int X, int Y)
{
     return    on_board(X + 1, Y + 2)
          + on_board(X + 2, Y + 1)
          + on_board(X - 1, Y + 2)
          + on_board(X - 2, Y + 1)
          + on_board(X + 1, Y - 2)
          + on_board(X + 2, Y - 1)
          + on_board(X - 1, Y - 2)
          + on_board(X - 2, Y - 1) ;
}


/* Print the board */
void Print_Board (int Board[][HEIGHT])
{
     int  X, Y;

     for (X = 0 ; X < WIDTH ; ++X) {
          for (Y = 0 ; Y < HEIGHT ; ++Y)
               printf("%3d", Board[X][Y]);
          putchar('\n');
     }
}
```

(13. continued)

```
/* Build the connectivity matrix for the chessboard */
Find_Connectivity (int Board[][HEIGHT])
{
      int  X, Y;

      for (X = 0 ; X < WIDTH ; ++X)
            for (Y = 0 ; Y < HEIGHT ; ++Y)
                  Board[X][Y] = Connectivity(X, Y);
}

main ()
{
      int  Board[WIDTH][HEIGHT];

      Find_Connectivity(Board);
      printf("\nConnectivity of board as seen by knight:\n");
      Print_Board(Board);
}
```

The following output was produced by the above program:

```
Connectivity of board as seen by knight:
    2   3   4   4   4   4   3   2
    3   4   6   6   6   6   4   3
    4   6   8   8   8   8   6   4
    4   6   8   8   8   8   6   4
    4   6   8   8   8   8   6   4
    4   6   8   8   8   8   6   4
    3   4   6   6   6   6   4   3
    2   3   4   4   4   4   3   2
```

```
14.   /* Find a kinght's tour on an 8x8 chessboard
       * using Warnsdorf's rule
       */
      #include <stdio.h>
      #define   HEIGHT    8
      #define   WIDTH     8

      /* prototypes for functions used from exercise #13 above */
      int  on_board (int, int);
      void Print_Board (int [][HEIGHT]);
      void Find_Connectivity (int [][HEIGHT]);
```

(14. continued)

```
/* find the adjacent square with smallest connectivity
 * takes current position in CurX, CurY, and updates
 * them to new position.
 * Returns 0 if all adjacent squares have been visited
 */
int next_pos (int Board[][HEIGHT], int Visited[][HEIGHT],
              int *CurX, int *CurY)
{
    int   min_conn = INT_MAX, /* smallest conn. so far */
          BestX, BestY,       /* position of min_conn */
          X, Y,               /* position we are checking */
          dX, dY;             /* offset for current pos */

    for (dX = 1 ; dX <= 2 ; ++dX) {
        dY = 3 - dX;
        do  {
            do  {
                X = *CurX + dX ; Y = *CurY + dY;
                if (on_board(X, Y) &&
                    (! Visited[X][Y]) &&
                    Board[X][Y] < min_conn) {
                    min_conn = Board[X][Y];
                    BestX = X;
                    BestY = Y;
                }
            } while ( (dX = -dX) < 0);
        } while ( (dY = -dY) < 0);
    }
    *CurX = BestX ; *CurY = BestY;
    /* we didn't find anyplace if min_conn unchanged */
    return (min_conn < INT_MAX);
}
```

(14. continued)

```c
/* decrement the connectivity for all squares adjacent
 * to a given square
 */
dec_conn (int Board[][8], int CurX, int CurY)
{
    int  dX, dY;

    for (dX = 1 ; dX <= 2 ; ++dX)  {
        dY = 3 - dX;
        do  {
            do {
                if (on_board(CurX + dX, CurY + dY))
                    -- Board[CurX + dX][CurY + dY];
            } while ( (dX = -dX) < 0);
        } while ( (dY = -dY) < 0);
    }
}

/* Read in a starting position and make sure it is valid */
void Read_Position (int *X, int *Y)
{
    for (;;) {
        scanf("%d%d", X, Y);
            /* convert to array subscript */
        --*X;  --*Y;
        if (on_board(*X, *Y))
            return;
        printf("Must be in range 1..8, 1..8:   ");
    }
}
```

(14. continued)

```
/* implement Warnsdorf's Rule by calling next_pos in a
 * loop until no unvisited adjacent squares are found.
 * This could be used starting at any position, but
 * only finds a complete tour starting from a corner.
 */
main ()
{
        /*steps to each square*/
        static int   Visited[WIDTH][HEIGHT];
        /* the connectivity matrix */
        int  Board[WIDTH][HEIGHT];
        int  CurX, CurY, nSteps = 0;

        printf("Knight's tour usng Warnsdorf's Rule\n");
        printf("Complete tour only if corner start.\n");
        printf("Enter starting position:  ");
        Read_Position(&CurX, &CurY);

        Find_Connectivity(Board);

        Visited[CurX][CurY] = ++nSteps;
        while (next_pos(Board, Visited, &CurX, &CurY)) {
                dec_conn(Board, CurX, CurY);
                Visited[CurX][CurY] = ++nSteps;
        }

        Print_Board(Visited);
}
```

The following is the output of the above program, with a starting position (1, 1) input.

```
Knight's tour usng Warnsdorf's Rule
Complete tour only if start at a corner.
Enter starting position: 1 1
  1 16 51 34  3 18 21 36
 50 33  2 17 52 35  4 19
 15 64 49 56 45 20 37 22
 32 55 44 63 48 53 42  5
 61 14 57 54 43 46 23 38
 28 31 62 47 58 41  6  9
 13 60 29 26 11  8 39 24
 30 27 12 59 40 25 10  7
```

15.
```c
/* Find a kinght's tour on an 8x8 chessboard
 * using Pohl's improvement to Warnsdorf's rule,
 * which is to break ties in minimum connectivity
 * recursively.  This is slower than the previous
 * exercise, due to the recursive tie-breaking.
 */
#include <stdio.h>
#include <limits.h>

#define    HEIGHT     8
#define    WIDTH      8

/* the connectivity matrix */
int   Board[WIDTH][HEIGHT];
/* # of steps to visit, 0 if non visited */
int   Visited[WIDTH][HEIGHT];

/* functions used from previous program: */
/* See if an (X, Y) coodinate is on the board */
int on_board (int X, int Y);

/* Check the connectivity for a given square */
int Connectivity (int X, int Y);

/* Print the board */
void Print_Board (int Board [] [HEIGHT]);

/* Build the connectivity matrix for the chessboard */
Find_Connectivity (int Board [] [HEIGHT]);

/* adjust the connectivity for all squares adjacent
 * to a given square
 */
adj_conn (int Board [] [HEIGHT],
          int CurX, int CurY, int Inc)
{
   int     dX, dY;

   for (dX = 1 ; dX <= 2 ; ++dX)  {
      dY = 3 - dX;
      do  {
         do {
            if (on_board(CurX + dX, CurY + dY))
               Board[CurX + dX][CurY + dY] += Inc;
         } while ( (dX = -dX) < 0);
      } while ( (dY = -dY) < 0);
   }
}
```

(15. continued)

```
/* Find the minimum connectivity possible after moving
 * given of steps from the given row, column position.
 * Takes current position in CurX, CurY, and updates
 * to new position.
 * Returns minimum connectivity.
 * Sets Tie to 1 if more than one position is minimum.
 */
int min_conn (int Depth, int CurX, int CurY, int *BestX,
              int *BestY, int *Tie)
{
  int    min = INT_MAX,     /* smallest conn. so far */
         X, Y,              /* position we are checking */
         dX, dY,            /* offset for current pos */
         conn, junk;

  /* base case of recursion just uses connectivity
   * of position we are at
   */
  if (Depth <= 0)
    return(Board[CurX][CurY]);

  for (dX = 1 ; dX <= 2 ; ++dX) {
    dY = 3 - dX; /* dY is 2 if dX is 1 & v.v. */
    do  {
      do  {
        X = CurX + dX ; Y = CurY + dY;
        if (on_board(X, Y) && (! Visited[X][Y])) {

          /* temporarily mark current pos as visited
           * to prevent loops
           */
          Visited[X][Y] = 1;
          adj_conn(Board, X, Y, -1);

          /* note we don't use X & Y position of min.
           * or tie on recursive calls
           */
          conn = min_conn(Depth-1, X, Y,
                          &junk, &junk, &junk);
          Visited[X][Y] = 0;
          adj_conn(Board, X, Y, 1);
```

(15. continued)

```
            if (conn < min && conn != -1) {
              min = conn;
              *BestX = X;
              *BestY = Y;
              *Tie = 0;
              }
            else if (conn == min)
              *Tie = 1;
          }
      } while ( (dX = -dX) < 0);
    } while ( (dY = -dY) < 0);
  }
  /* note if did not find any unvisited squares
   * then connectivity is zero.
   */
  return ((min == INT_MAX) ? 0 : min);
}

/* Move to the adjacent position with minimum connectivity.
 * Although the tie-breaking algorithm is recursive,
 * we won't know if there is a tie until we have
 * looked at all immediate neighbors of the knight.
 * Thus we iterate on Depth, which is the maximum
 * level of recursive tie-breaking, and allow
 * one extra level of recursion each time.
 * According to Pohl's 1967 article referenced in
 * the exercise, on an 8x8 board we never actually
 * have to go more than Depth = 2.  But the algorith,
 * here, because of symmetry of the board, will
 * pursue ties to depth 8 occasionally.
 * In the limit, Depth would equal the total length
 * of the kngiht's tour, and we would have done the
 * entire knight's tour within the tie-breaking.
 */
next_pos (int *CurX, int *CurY)
{
    int   BestX, BestY, Depth = 1, Tie;

  /* stop looping when no tie or when connectivity 0 reached */
    for (Depth = 1;
        min_conn(Depth, *CurX, *CurY, &BestX, &BestY, &Tie)
          && Tie;
        ++Depth)
    ;
  *CurX = BestX; *CurY = BestY;
}
```

(15. continued)

```
    /* Read in a starting position and make sure it is valid */
    void Read_Position (int *X, int *Y)
    {
        for (;;) {
            scanf("%d%d", X, Y);
            --*X; --*Y; /* convert to array subscript */
            if (on_board(*X, *Y))
                return;
            printf("Must be in range 1..8, 1..8:  ");
        }
    }

    main ()
    {
        int  CurX, CurY, Step = 0;

        printf("Knight's tour usng Pohl's improvement");
        printf(" to Warnsdorf's Rule0);
        printf("Enter starting position:  ");
        Read_Position(&CurX, &CurY);
        Find_Connectivity(Board);

        for (Step = 1 ; Step <= HEIGHT * WIDTH ; ++Step) {
            Visited[CurX][CurY] = nSteps;
            next_pos(&CurX, &CurY);
            adj_conn(Board, CurX, CurY, -1);
        }
        Print_Board(Visited);
    }
```

The following output demonstrates the difference between the two algorithms. The first column is the output of Pohl's modification to Warnsdorf's algorithm, and the second column is the output of the unmodified Warnsdorf algorithm. Note in particular the third and fourth cases, where the unmodified algorithm fails to find a complete tour (as indicated by the zeroes). The first two cases start at a corner square, and both algorithms produce the same result. The last case starts at an interior square, and both algorithms manage to find a complete tour, although they are different.

Starting at position 1, 1:

```
 1 40 25 10 45  6 27  8        1 16 51 34  3 18 21 36
24 11  2 63 26  9 46  5       50 33  2 17 52 35  4 19
39 64 41 44  3 58  7 28       15 64 49 56 45 20 37 22
12 23 62 57 42 47  4 55       32 55 44 63 48 53 42  5
61 38 43 48 59 56 29 18       61 14 57 54 43 46 23 38
22 13 60 35 32 19 54 51       28 31 62 47 58 41  6  9
37 34 15 20 49 52 17 30       13 60 29 26 11  8 39 24
14 21 36 33 16 31 50 53       30 27 12 59 40 25 10  7
```

Starting at position 8, 1:

```
30 27 12 47 40 25 10  7       30 27 12 63 40 25 10  7
13 46 29 26 11  8 39 24       13 64 29 26 11  8 39 24
28 31 62 45 48 41  6  9       28 31 58 45 62 41  6  9
61 14 49 56 59 44 23 38       57 14 61 52 55 44 23 38
32 55 60 63 50 57 42  5       32 53 56 59 46 51 42  5
15 64 51 58 43 20 37 22       15 60 47 54 43 20 37 22
54 33  2 17 52 35  4 19       48 33  2 17 50 35  4 19
 1 16 53 34  3 18 21 36        1 16 49 34  3 18 21 36
```

Starting at position 3, 3:

```
21 18 49 62 23  8  3  6       35 20  3 38 31 22  5  8
50 63 22 19  2  5 24  9        2 39 36 21  4  7 30 23
17 20  1 48 61 26  7  4       19 34  1 50 37 32  9  6
64 51 54 27 36 59 10 25       40 49  0 33 60 51 24 29
55 16 47 60 53 28 35 38        0 18 41 48  0 28 55 10
46 43 52 29 58 37 32 11       42 15  0 59 56 47 52 25
15 56 41 44 13 30 39 34       17 58 13 44 27 54 11 46
42 45 14 57 40 33 12 31       14 43 16 57 12 45 26 53
```

Starting at position 6, 6:

```
15 18 13 32 43 20 37 34        0 14 41 48  0 16 39 36
12 31 16 19 36 33 42 21       42 47  0 15 40 37  0 17
17 14 29 44 41 58 35 38       13  0 49 46  0  0 35 38
30 11 60 57 50 39 22 55       50 43 30  0 54 45 18  0
61 28 45 40 59 56 49  2       27 12 51 44 29  0 53 34
10  7 62 51 46  1 54 23        6  9 28 31 52  1 22 19
27 64  5  8 25 52  3 48       11 26  7  4 21 24 33  2
 6  9 26 63  4 47 24 53        8  5 10 25 32  3 20 23
```

Starting at position 4, 7:

```
30 27 10 61 24  3  8  5        8  5 10 25 32  3 20 23
11 60 29 26  9  6 23  2       11 26  7  4 21 24 33  2
28 31 56 59 62 25  4  7        6  9 28 31 50 35 22 19
55 12 63 42 49 58  1 22       27 12 51 36 29 46  1 34
32 43 50 57 64 41 18 47       52 37 30 49 64 59 18 47
13 54 35 44 51 48 21 40       13 40 55 60 45 48 63 58
36 33 52 15 38 19 46 17       38 53 42 15 56 61 44 17
53 14 37 34 45 16 39 20       41 14 39 54 43 16 57 62
```

CHAPTER 13

STRUCTURES AND LINKED LISTS

A lot of interesting projects and classroom examples become possible once structures are introduced. The first programming project for this chapter is a reasonably functional data base. Endless variations on this theme are possible, as the data format can be easily changed. If class format and resources permit, the students can be given the freedom to design a data base format of their own choosing, making the project more interesting. The programming projects in the next chapter will build on this data base program, extending it to include storage of the data base in a disk file.

TRANSPARENCY MASTERS

Declaring structures
Accessing a structure member
Declarations and assignments; an example
Operator precedence and associativity
Example data structure: student records
The use of `typedef`
Self-referential structures
Linear linked lists
Dynamic memory allocation
Create a list by recursion
Inserting into a linked list
Deleting from a linked list

ANSWERS TO EXERCISES

1. The tag name of the structure is "food". The array declaration would be:

```
struct food    meal [10];
```

The assignments to an array element would be:

```
strcpy(meal[0].name, "apple");
meal[0].portion_weight = 4;
meal[0].calories = 200;
```

2.
```
/* Program to compute calories in a meal */

#include <stdio.h>

#define   N_FOODS   10        /* # of items in a meal */

struct food {
   char   name[15];
   int    portion_weight, calories;
};

struct food    meal[N_FOODS];

main ()
{
   int    i, tot_calories = 0;

   printf("Today's menu and calorie count:\n");
   printf("%15s%5s\n", "food item:", "calories");
   for (i = 0 ; i < N_FOODS ; ++i)   {
      printf("%15s%5d\n", meal[i].name,
                          meal[i].calories);
      tot_calories += meal[i].calories;
   }
   printf("Total calories    %5d\n", tot_calories);
}
```

3. The function will compile without error, but will not run correctly because the pointer variable `c_ptr` is never initialized with a pointer to an actual card struct. Either `malloc` or an assignment of a declared card struct must be used.

4. The following functions will sort and print restaurants by average cost.

```
/* struct definition to describe a restaurant */
struct restaurant  {
    char        name[15];
    char        address[40];
    float       average_cost;
    char        food_type[10];
};

/* array of restaurant structures */
struct restaurant   rest_list[N_RESTAURANTS];

/* Sort the array by average cost */
void sort_rest_list (struct restaurant list[], int n)
{
    int     i,j;
    struct restaurant       temp;

    for (i = 0 ; i < n - 1 ; ++i)
        for (j = n - 1 ; i < j ; --j)
            if (list[j-1].average_cost
                > list[j].average_cost)  {
                temp = list[j-1];
                list[j-1] = list[j];
                list[j] = temp;
            }
}

/* print restaurants of a given type
 * in order of average cost
 */
void print_rest_type (struct restaurant list[],
                        int size, char *type)
{
    int     i;

    sort_rest_list(list, size);

    for (i = 0 ; i < size ; ++i)
        if (strcmp(list[i].food_type, type) == 0)
            printf("%15s%10.2f\n", list[i].name,
                                list[i].average_cost);
}
```

5. The following program deals and sorts a hand of five playing cards.

```c
/*  Arrange and print out a hand of five cards
 *  in order of ascending pips value
 */
#include <stdio.h>

/* structure to define a playing card */
enum suit_type {clubs, diamonds, hearts, spades};

enum pips_type {deuce = 2, trey, four, five, six,
                seven, eight, nine, ten, jack,
            queen, king, ace};

struct card {
    enum pips_type pips;
    enum suit_type suit;
};

/* arrays of strings to hold name for suits and pips */
char * suit_name [] = {"clubs", "diamonds",
                        "hearts", "spades"};
char * pips_name [] = {NULL, NULL, "deuce",
                        "three", "four", "five",
                "six", "seven", "eight",
                "nine", "ten", "jack",
                "queen", "king", "ace"};

/* sort a hand of cards by pips value, using bubblesort */
void sort_hand (struct card hand[], int size)
{
    int    i, j;
    struct card temp;

    for (i = 0 ; i < size - 1 ; ++i)
        for (j = size - 1 ; i < j ; --j)
            if (hand[j-1].pips > hand[j].pips)  {
                temp = hand[j-1];
                hand[j-1] = hand[j];
                hand[j] = temp;
            }
}
```

(5. continued)

```
/* print a hand of cards */
void print_hand (struct card hand[], int size)
{
    int  i;

    for (i = 0 ; i < size ; ++i)
        printf("%10s%12s\n",
                pips_name[hand[i].pips],
                suit_name[hand[i].suit]);
}

/* for this demonstration program, we just initialize
 * the hand with 5 arbitrary cards, sort, and print.
 */

/* array to hold a hand of five cards */
#define        HAND_SIZE        5
struct card    Poker_Hand[5] = { {deuce, diamonds},
                                    {ace, clubs},
                                {seven, spades},
                            {ace, spades},
                            {deuce, hearts}};

main ()
{
    sort_hand(Poker_Hand, HAND_SIZE);
    print_hand(Poker_Hand, HAND_SIZE);
}
```

6. The following program computes and prints the average grade for each student in an array of structures.

```
/* Print average grade for each student */
#include "student.h"

struct student_data class_list[CLASS_SIZE];

/* return the numeric value of a letter grade */
int Numeric_Grade (char Letter_Grade)
{
    return Letter_Grade >= 'A' && Letter_Grade <= 'D' ?
            4 - (Letter_Grade - 'A') : 0 ;
}

/* compute the average for a single student */
int Average_Grade (struct student_data *Student,
                    int num_courses)
{
    int    i, Tot_Score = 0;

    for (i = 0 ; i < num_courses ; ++i)
        Tot_Score += Numeric_Grade(Student -> grade [i]);

    return(Tot_Score / num_courses);
}

/* Print name and average for each student in a class */
void Print_Class_List (struct student_data *Class,
                        int size)
{
    int i;

    for (i = 0 ; i < size ; ++i)
        printf("%20s%5.1f\n", Class[i].p.name,
                Average_Grade(& Class[i], NCOURSES));
}
```

7. This program sorts the student list by birthdate. NOTE: For this exercise we have modified the `struct date` to store the month as an integer instead of as a character string; otherwise the sorting algorithm becomes complex and inefficient. In practice a alphanumeric month would be converted into an integer month number first, and then the sort given here would be applied

```c
/* Program to sort a student list by date, oldest fist
 * The header "student.h" is written here instead of
 * "#include"d, as we have modified the date structure
 */
#include <stdio.h>

#define   CLASS_SIZE     50
#define   NCOURSES  10

struct date {
     short     day;
     short     month;
     short     year;
};

struct personal {
     char name[20];
     struct    date birthday;
};

struct student_data {
     struct personal     p;
     int          student_id;
     char         grade[NCOURSES];
};

/* array of students */
struct student_data student_list[CLASS_SIZE];

/* function to compare two student's birthday
 * returns 0 if equal, positive if first is older,
 *        negative if second is older
 * the actual parameters are just the date structures
 * and are passed by reference for efficiency
 */
int compare_dates (struct date *date1,
                   struct date *date2)
{
     if (date1 -> year != date2 -> year)
        return date1 -> year - date2 -> year;
     if (date1 -> month != date2 -> month)
        return date1 -> month - date2 -> month;
     return date1 -> day - date2 -> day;
}
```

(7. continued)

```c
/* Exchange two student records */
void Swap (struct student_data *S1,
           struct student_data *S2)
{
    struct student_data temp;

    temp = *S1;
    *S1 = *S2;
    *S2 = temp;
}

/* Bubble sort the student array by date
 * into ASCENDING order
 */
void bubble (struct student_data A[], int class_size)
{
    int    i, j, Changed = 1;

    for (i = 0 ; (i < class_size - 1) && Changed ; ++i) {
        Changed = 0;
        for (j = class_size - 1 ; i < j ; --j)
            if (compare_dates(&A[j - 1].p.birthday,
                              &A[j].p.birthday) < 0) {
                Changed = 1;
                Swap(&A[j - 1], &A[j]);
            }
    }
}

/* Print out a date record.  The actual parameter
 * is passed by reference for efficiency
 */
void print_date (struct date *D)
{
    printf("%d/%d/%d", D -> month, D -> day, D -> year);
}
```

(7. continued)

```c
/* Print out the student list */
void print_student_list (struct student_data list[],
                         int size)
{
    int  i;

    for (i = 0 ; i < size ; ++i) {
        printf("%20s", list[i].p.name);
        print_date(& list[i].p.birthday);
        putchar('\n');
    }
}

/* Sort the student list by birthday, and print */
void sort_and_print (struct student_data list[],
                     int size)
{
    bubble(list, size);
    print_student_list(list, size);
}
```

8.
```c
/* Print a student record in a nice format */
#include <stdio.h>
#include "student.h"

void prn_student_data (struct student_data *S)
{
    int        i;

    printf("Student #%d    %s\n",
            S -> student_id, (S -> p).name);
    printf("Birthday:  %s %d, %d\n",
          (S -> p).birthday.month,
          (S -> p).birthday.day,
          (S -> p).birthday.year);
    printf("Grades: ");
    for (i = 0 ; i < NCOURSES ; ++i)
       printf("  %c", S -> grade[i]);
    putchar('\n');
}
```

9.
```c
/*  Program to generate balanced menus
 *  Stores a database of foods containing name,
 * calories, *  food type, and cost.  The data is input
 * from the user and stored in an array of structs.
 * The program then systematically selects all
 * combinations of four foods of different types and
 * meeting maximum cost and minimum and maximum calorie
 * constraints.  In a "real" application, the food data
 * base would be in an external data file, but it
 * exists here in the form of an initializer on the
 * array of structs, thus leaving stdin free for
 * ineractive use.  Repeats as long as user desires.
 */
#include <stdio.h>

#define   MAXFOODS  100

/* The food struct definition */
struct food {
    char        name[20];
    int         cals;          /* calories per serving */
    float  cost;         /* cost per serving */
    char        type;          /* food type code */
};

/* Print a menu */
Print_Menu (struct food db[],
            int item1, int item2, int item3, int item4)
{
    printf("%s; %s; %s; %s.\n",
            db[item1].name, db[item2].name,
            db[item3].name, db[item4].name);
}
```

(9. continued)

```
/* the data base: */
struct food    db[] =
       { {"Milk, whole", 150, 0.25, 'D'},
         {"Milk, nonfat", 85, 0.35, 'D'},
         {"Cheese, cheddar", 115, 0.50, 'D'},
         {"Eggs, medium", 80, 0.25, 'D'},
         {"Beef, roast", 165, 1.00, 'M'},
         {"Beef, corned", 185, 0.75, 'M'},
         {"Ham, baked", 245, 1.00, 'M'},
         {"Pork, roast", 310, 1.00, 'M'},
         {"Lamb, roast", 130, 1.00, 'M'},
         {"Chicken, broiler", 240, 0.80, 'M'},
         {"Fish, baked", 135, 0.75, 'M'},
         {"Tuna", 170, 0.50, 'M'},
         {"Liver", 195, 1.00, 'M'},
         {"Asparagus", 30, 0.50, 'V'},
         {"Beans, lima", 170, 0.50, 'V'},
         {"Beans, snap", 30, 0.25, 'V'},
         {"Beans, baked", 310, 0.30, 'V'},
         {"Broccoli", 40, 0.40, 'V'},
         {"Cabbage, cooked", 20, 0.20, 'V'},
         {"Carrots, cooked", 50, 0.25, 'V'},
         {"Corn, ear", 70, 0.50, 'V'},
         {"Lettuce", 5, 0.20, 'V'},
         {"Mushrooms", 20, 0.50, 'V'},
         {"Peppers", 15, 0.35, 'V'},
         {"Potato, baked", 145, 0.30, 'V'},
         {"Spinach, cooked", 40, 0.40, 'V'},
         {"Tomato, raw", 25, 0.30, 'V'},
         {"Ketchup", 15, 0.10, 'V'},
         {"Apples", 80, 0.30, 'V'},
         {"Banana, medium", 100, 0.40, 'V'},
         {"Orange, medium", 65, 0.40, 'V'},
         {"Strawberries", 55, 0.80, 'V'},
         {"Biscuit", 105, 0.30, 'G'},
         {"Bread, whole", 65, 0.15, 'G'},
         {"Bread, white", 70, 0.10, 'G'},
         {"Bran, flakes", 105, 0.20, 'G'},
         {"Oatmeal", 130, 0.30, 'G'},
         {"Butter", 35, 0.10, 'D'} };

#define   NFOODS    (sizeof(db) / sizeof (struct food))
```

(9. continued)

```
/* Construct a meal.  Enumerate over all distinct
 * combinations of four food items. Distinctness is
 * guaranteed by starting each search through the
 * array from the index where the last one left off
 * For each combination of four foods, check for four
 * distinct types, and calorie and cost constraints.
 * Print out each menu which satisfies all conditions.
 * Keep going to next one if user enters RETURN
 */
void Find_Menus (struct food db[], float Max_Cost,
           int Max_Cals, int Min_Cals, int nFoods)
{
  int      item1, item2, item3, item4, Cals;
  float    Cost;

  /* choose first item */
  for (item1 = 0 ; item1 < nFoods ; ++item1)
    /* choose second item */
    for (item2 = item1 + 1 ; item2 < nFoods ; ++item2)
      /* check for different type */
      if (db[item1].type != db[item2].type)
        /* choose third item */
        for (item3 = item2 + 1 ; item3 < nFoods ; ++item3)
          /* check for third item different types */
          if (db[item3].type != db[item2].type &&
              db[item3].type != db[item1].type)
            /* choose fourth item */
            for (item4 = item3 + 1 ;item4 < nFoods ;++item4)
              /* check for different types */
              if (db[item4].type != db[item3].type &&
                  db[item4].type != db[item2].type &&
                  db[item4].type != db[item1].type) {
                /* check cost and calorie constraints */
                Cost = db[item1].cost + db[item2].cost +
                       db[item3].cost + db[item4].cost;
                Cals = db[item1].cals + db[item2].cals +
                       db[item3].cals + db[item4].cals;
                if (Cals <= Max_Cals && Cals >= Min_Cals
                    && Cost <= Max_Cost) {
                  /* print one if found */
                  Print_Menu(db,item1,item2,item3,item4);
                  printf("RETURN for another or EOF");
                  if (getchar() == EOF)
                    exit(0);
                }
              }
  printf("No more menu possibilities.\n");
}
```

(9. continued)

```
main ()
{
      int  Max_Cals, Min_Cals;
      float     Max_Cost;

      printf("Enter maximum calories: ");
      scanf("%d", &Max_Cals);
      printf("Enter minimum calories: ");
      scanf("%d", &Min_Cals);
      printf("Enter maximum cost: ");
      scanf("%f", &Max_Cost);

      Find_Menus(db, Max_Cost, Max_Cals, Min_Cals, NFOODS);
}
```

10. You can't have one structure which contains another structure which in turn contains the first -- it's physically impossible. The problem can be solved by using pointers. The husband and wife can point to each other, but they can't contain each other:

```
struct husband  {
   char         name[10];
   int          age;
   struct wife *spouse;
} a;

struct wife  {
   char         name[10];
   int          age;
   struct husband   *wife;
} b;
```

11.
```
/* Transform an array to a linear linked list,
 * and count the number of people above a given age
 * and above a given weight.  Note this file contains
 * the information in list.h instead of #including it.
 */

struct s_data {
    char    name[10];
    int     age;
    int     weight;
} ;

typedef    struct s_data   DATA;

struct linked_list  {
    DATA            d;
    struct linked_list    *next;
};

typedef    struct linked_list   ELEMENT;
typedef    ELEMENT *        LINK;

/* Create a list from an array, returns pointer
 * to head of list.  We read the array backwards
 * and construct the linked list backwards so it
 * comes out forwards.
 */
LINK create_list (DATA A[], int n)
{
    LINK    list_head = null, new_rec;

    while (--n >= 0)  {
        /* allocate a new record */
        new_rec = malloc(sizeof (ELEMENT));
        /* copy data to element */
        new_rec -> d = A[n];
        /* link to previous element */
        new_rec -> next = list_head;
        /* now this is first element */
        list_head = new_rec;
    }
    return list_head;
}
```

(11. continued)

```
/* Count the number of individuals in a linked
 * list above both a given age and a given weight.
 */
int count_list (LINK p, int Given_Age, int Given_Weight)
{
    int    Count = 0;

    while (p)  {
        if (p -> d . age > Given_Age &&
            p -> d . weight > Given_Weight)
          ++Count;
        p = p -> next;
    }
    return Count;
}
```

12.
```
/* Two functions to sort a linked list
 * The transposition sort presented in exercise 11
 * of chapter 9 is used instead of bubble sort because
 * we can only move forward in a singly linked list.
 * Note the list head must be passed by reference
 * since the first element of the list might be changed.
 */
```

```c
/* Function to exchange two list elements
 * given pointers to element one before each element
 * to exchange.   The list head is passed by reference
 * in case the first list element is changed.
 * The pointers pi and pj are also passed by reference, since
 * they must themselves be swapped for the main program.
 */
void swap_elements (LINK *list_head_ptr,
                    LINK lastpi, LINK lastpj,
               LINK *pi_ptr, LINK *pj_ptr)
{
     LINK  temp, pi = *pi_ptr, pj = *pj_ptr;

   /* It turns out that if the elements to be swapped
    * are next to each other, it has to be handled
    * as a special case
    */
   if (lastpi == pj) {    /* pi follows pj */
      if (lastpj == NULL)
         *list_head_ptr = pi;
      else
         lastpj -> next = pi;
      pj -> next = pi -> next;
      pi -> next = pj;
   }
   else if (lastpj == pi) {  /* pj follows pi */
      if (lastpi == NULL)
         *list_head_ptr = pj;
      else
         lastpi -> next = pj;
      pi -> next = pj -> next;
      pj -> next = pi;
   }
   else {       /* neither pi nor pj follows the other */
      if (lastpi == NULL)
         *list_head_ptr = pj;
      else
         lastpi -> next = pj;
      if (lastpj == NULL)
         *list_head_ptr = pi;
      else
         lastpj -> next = pi;
      temp = pi -> next;
      pi -> next = pj -> next;
      pj -> next = temp;
   }
   /* Now swap the original pi and pj */
   *pi_ptr = pj;
   *pj_ptr = pi;
```

(12. continued)

```
void sort_by_age (LINK *list_head_ptr)
{
    LINK   pi, pj, lastpi, lastpj ;

    pi = *list_head_ptr;
    /* null backlink shows head of list */
    lastpi = NULL;
    while (pi != NULL) {
        pj = pi -> next;
        lastpj = pi;
        while (pj != NULL) {
            if (pi -> d.age > pj -> d.age)
                swap_elements(list_head_ptr, lastpi, lastpj,
                            &pi, &pj);
            lastpj = pj;
            pj = pj -> next;
            }
        lastpi = pi;
        pi = pi -> next;
        }
}

void sort_by_name (LINK *list_head_ptr)
{
    LINK   pi, pj, lastpi, lastpj ;

    pi = *list_head_ptr;
    /* null backlink shows head of list */
    lastpi = NULL;
    while (pi != NULL) {
        pj = pi -> next;
        lastpj = pi;
        while (pj != NULL) {
            if (strcmp(pi -> d.name, pj -> d.name) > 0)
                swap_elements(list_head_ptr, lastpi, lastpj,
            &pi, &pj);
            lastpj = pj;
            pj = pj -> next;
            }
        lastpi = pi;
        pi = pi -> next;
        }
}
```

13.    ```c
/* Iterative function to count the elements
 * in a linear linked list
 */

#include "list.h"

int Count (LINK head)
{
    int   n = 0;

    while (head) {
        ++n;
        head = head -> next;
    }
    return n;
}
```

14.    ```c
/* Insert an element at the first position following
 * an element containing a given DATA item, or at end
 * of list if not found.
 */

#include "list.h"

/* iterative version of lookup function from the text */
LINK lookup(DATA c, LINK head)
{
    while (head && head -> d != c)
        head = head -> next;
    return head;
}

/* function to return a pointer to last element in a list,
 * in case lookup returns null
 * returns null if list is empty
 */
LINK last_element (LINK head)
{
    if (head)
        while (head -> next)
            head = head -> next;
    return head;
}
```

(14. continued)

```
    /* insert a new element containing "new_data" following
     * element containing "old_data", or at end of list
     * the list head is passed by reference in case the
     * list starts out null
     */
    void insert_after (LINK *head_ptr,
                        DATA old_data, DATA new_data)
    {
        LINK   back_ptr, new_el;

        /* find pointer to one before new element */
        back_ptr = lookup(old_data, *head_ptr);
        if (! back_ptr)
            back_ptr = last_element(*head_ptr);

        /* set up the new element */
        new_el = malloc(sizeof (ELEMENT));
        if (! back_ptr)  {
            /* list was empty, new element is now
             * only element in list
             */
            new_el -> next = NULL;
            *head_ptr = new_el;
        }
        else  {
            /* list not empty */
            new_el -> next = back_ptr -> next;
            back_ptr -> next = new_el;
        }
    }
```

15. The parentheses are necessary because the dereferencing operator "*" has lower precedence than the member accessing operator ".". Without the parentheses, it will try to get a member of the pointer before dereferencing it. This will not compile.

17. In the `insert` function, if `p1` and `p2` are not pointers to adjacent elements, the list structure will be corrupted. If the element pointed to by `p2` happens to come after `p1` in the list, the elements between `p1` and `p2` will be lost. If `p2` happens to come before `p1` in the list, the list will be linked in a loop.

18. The two structures may require different amounts of memory on computers which require words to be aligned on a word boundary. This forces the compiler to insert "holes" or unused bytes in the struct. On a 16-bit machine which requires words to be on an even address, the first structure will require 4 bytes, and the second 6 bytes. On a 32-bit machine which requires words to be on an address which is a multiple of 4, the first structure will require 6 bytes, and the second 12.

19. Both commas inside the for-loop are comma operators; those in the declaration and the printf statement are not. One way to rewrite the code without any comma operators is the following:

```
int   i, j;

i = 0;
j = 1;
while (i < LIMIT)   {
      printf("%12d%12d\n", i, j);
      i += 2;
      j += 2;
}
```

PROGRAMMING PROJECT 13-1

Purpose: structs, data bases, more practice with strings.

Although modern data base systems use quite complex data structures, a data base in its simplest form is just an array of structs. It can be viewed as a table in which the rows are the individual items or structs in the data base and the columns are the members of each struct. This project involves a database which might be used by a library to automate its card catalog of books, allowing on-line searches for books by a particular author or subject. Information about each book is stored in a struct. The members are Title, Author, Keyword List, and Location, all of which are strings. The listing for this data base will contain one row for each book, and columns for Title, Author, etc. The program will present the following menu:

```
Enter:
N    Enter new book
L    List catalog of books
A    Find book by author
K    Find book by subject keyword
Q    Quit program.
```

The program will use an array of structs, and also a count of how many books have been entered, i.e. how many locations in the array are actually in use. Use 40 as the maximum length for the Title, Author, and Keyword List components, and 10 for the Location.

The N option will prompt for each component of the new struct in turn, and increment the count of books entered. If this count exceeds the size of the array (use 20 for this exercise) an error message is displayed instead. (Remember that you can input directly into a member of a struct in an array, without using a temporary variable.)

The L option will print column titles and then one line for each struct. To keep the display to one line per book, only show the first 20 characters of the Author, Title, and Keyword List members. The A option will prompt for a string (terminated by newline) and look through each struct in the data base for ones with matching author member. Note there may be more than one match, and all are printed. Output format is the same as for List.

One problem with string look-up in data bases is that the user may not remember the entire string or the exact spelling. Therefore this program, like many database systems, uses "substring matching" (provided by the standard library function strstr) instead of the string equality function strcmp. The substring match strstr(*string1, string2*) is "true" if *string2* occurs as a sub-string anywhere within *string1*. For example, an author entry such as "Pohl, Ira and Al Kelley" (as *string1*) would be matched by substrings (as *string2*) "Pohl" or "Kelley" (and even by "Al" and "Ira", although the number of extraneous matches will tend to increase as the length of the substring decreases). Substring matching is especially useful with subject lookup. The Keyword List component contains a list of words, separated by spaces, describing the topic of the book. The user only needs to enter one keyword, and the substring matching will find any entries containing that keyword anywhere in the Keyword List component.

PROGRAMMING PROJECT 13-2

Purpose: structs, linked lists, more practice with strings.

Although modern data base systems use quite complex data structures, a data base in its simplest form is just a list of structs. It can be viewed as a table in which the rows are the individual items or structs in the data base and the columns are the components of each struct. This assignment involves a database of names, addresses, and telephone numbers. The database is to be implemented as a linked list of structs. This implementation allows for efficient deletion of structs from the data base, and avoids having a limit on the maximum size of the data base which would be the case if an array were used instead.

Information about each person is stored in a struct. The members are Name, Address, and Telephone Number, all of which are strings. The listing for this data base will contain one row for each entry, and columns for the Name, Address, and Phone Number.

The program will be menu-driven as before, and will present the following menu:

```
Enter:
N    New entry
L    List database
F    Find entry by name
D    Delete entry
Q    Quit program
```

Use 40 as the maximum length for the Name and Address components, and 16 for the Phone #.

The N option will prompt for each component of the new struct in turn, and increment the count of people entered. (Remember that you can input directly into a component of a struct in a list, without using a temporary variable.)

The L option will print column titles and then one line for each struct. To keep the display to one line per entry, only show the first 20 characters of the Name and Address components.

The N option will prompt for a string (terminated by newline) and look through each struct in the data base for ones with matching Name component. Note there may be more than one match, and all are printed. Output format is the same as for List.

One problem with string look-up in data bases is that the user may not remember the entire string or the exact spelling. Therefore this program, like many database systems, uses "substring matching" (provided by the standard library function **strstr**) instead of the string equality function **strcmp**. The substring match **strstr(string1, string2)** is "true" if **string2** occurs as a sub-string anywhere within **string1**. For example, a Name entry such as "Robert Stevens" (as **string1**) would be matched by substrings (as **string2**) "Stevens", "Robert", or "Rob".

The D command for Delete prompts for the Name of the struct to be deleted. An entry in the array is deleted by linking around it and using `free()` to release its storage.

CHAPTER 14

INPUT/OUTPUT AND FILES

I like to start out by pointing out that everyone in the class has been using files all quarter (or semester), since that is how a program is stored. The only difference now is that they will be manipulating files from within a program.

- Go over the difference between using redirection on the command line and opening a file from within a program -- the latter allows you to have more than one file open for input or output, and still use the terminal for message I/O.

- The basic sequence of operations in file processing -- opening, reading/writing, and closing. I explain this process first in general terms, and then introduce the C library functions.

- I like to present the reading and writing of data to/from a file in terms of three levels -- the formatted (fscanf/fprintf) I/O at the highest level, which is exactly like scanf/printf for terminal I/O which they have been using all along; the line-by-line I/O (gets/puts) in the middle level; and the character-by-character I/O (getc/putc) at the lowest level, which is just like getchar/putchar.

- Emphasize the necessity for error checking, especially on opening a file. Unlike declared variables which exist within the program, files are external to the program and you can't be sure a file is even there. Errors in file I/O are much more common than internal program errors. Also, caution students that errors in writing a file can destroy useful data.

- A point which often trips up students is the necessity of checking for end of file on input. Neglecting to do this will often result in a program getting stuck in an infinite loop at the end.

There are numerous library functions for handling files in the C library, and students cannot be expected to memorize the entire list, along with the parameters for each. They should, be aware of what is available and where to look up detailed information. The testbank questions for this chapter test the students' knowledge of fopen, ..., but do not test the detailed calling sequence for these functions. I usually don't cover random file access in detail, just mention that it can be done and the library functions involved.

Similarly, there are numerous options for the control string used by scanf, printf, and other functions for formatted input/output. The testbank questions cover the %d, %f, %e, %s, and %c conversions, with both field length and precision, as well as the scan set (%[...]) conversion and the effect of "ordinary characters" in the control string.

TRANSPARENCY MASTERS

printf conversions
Examples of printf conversions -- numeric
Examples of printf conversions -- text
scanf conversions #1
scanf conversions #2
Some examples of scanf conversions
Opening a file
Example: double spacing a file
Random access in a file

ANSWERS TO EXERCISES

```
1.      /* Read lines from a file named on the command line,
         * and print every other line to stdout
         * uses [^\n] control string
         */
        #include <stdio.h>

        /* copy every other line from opened file to stdout */
        void copy_alternate_lines (FILE *fp)
        {
            char    Line[256];      /*256 is unix max for lines*/
            int     Line_Count = 0;

            *Line = '\0';   /* in case fscanf fails (blank line) */
            while (fscanf(fp, " %256[^\n]", Line) != EOF) {
                /* increment line, test for odd */
                if (++Line_Count & 1)
                    printf("%s\n", Line);
                getc(fp);       /* skip the newline */
                *Line = '\0';   /* in case fscanf fails next time */
            }
        }

        main (int argc, char **argv)
        {
            FILE    *fp;

            if (argc < 2)
                printf("File name must be in command line.\n");
            else if ((fp = fopen(argv[1], "r")) == NULL)
                printf("Cannot open file %s.\n", argv[1]);
            else copy_alternate_lines(fp);
        }
```

4. The code prints only the third out of every four lines input. The other three lines are read with `%*[^\n]` which has the "assignment suppression" symbol `*`.

5. File `tmp1` gets the string `aaa`, and file `tmp2` gets the string `abc`. The `sscanf` in the first `for` loop uses the constant pointer `s`, which points to the first character of the string at each iteration of the loop. The `sscanf` in the second `for` loop uses the string pointer `p` which is incremented each time through the loop and so gets a different character each time.

6. If you redirect standard output to a file, the line `and alphabet pie` is printed on the display, since `stderr` is not redirected. If both `stdout` and `stderr` are redirected to a file, both lines will be written to the file, although not necessarily in the order shown.

7.
```
      /* Number the lines in a file.
       * File name passed on command line.
       */
      #include <stdio.h>

      /* Pick up command line argument and open file by that
       * name.  Return file pointer if successful,
       * NULL if not.
       */
      FILE * Get_File (int argc, char **argv)
      {
          FILE    *fp = NULL;

          if (argc < 2)
              printf("File name must be on command line.\n");
          else if (! (fp = fopen(argv[1], "r")))
              printf("Cannot open file %s.\n", argv[1]);
          return(fp);
      }
```

```
/* Copy lines from given file to stdout,
 * with line numbers prepended
 */
void Number_Lines (FILE *fp)
{
    char    Line[256];
    int     Line_Counter;

    *Line = '\0';    /* in case fscanf fails (blank line) */
    for (Line_Counter = 1 ;
         fscanf(fp, "%256[^\n]", Line) != EOF ;
       ++Line_Counter) {
      printf("%d %s\n", Line_Counter, Line);
      getc(fp);     /* skip the newline */
      *Line = '\0';   /* in case fscanf fails next time */
    }
}

main (int argc, char **argv)
{
    FILE    *fp;
    if (fp = Get_File(argc, argv))
        Number_Lines(fp);
}
```

8.
```
/* Number the lines in a file. File name passed on
 * command line.  The program first counts the number
 * of lines in the file so that line numbers can be
 * right-justified in a constant field width.
 */
#include <stdio.h>

/* Pick up command line argument and open file by that
 * name.  Return file pointer if successful, NULL if not
 */
FILE * Get_File (int argc, char **argv)
{
    FILE    *fp = NULL;

    if (argc < 2)
       printf("File name must be on command line.\n");
    else if (! (fp = fopen(argv[1], "r")))
       printf("Cannot open file %s.\n", argv[1]);
    return(fp);
}
```

(8. continued)

```c
/* Return the number of lines in a file.  Note the
 * number of lines is just the number of newlines.
 */
int Count_Lines (FILE *fp)
{
    int      Counter = 0, Ch;

    while ((Ch = getc(fp)) != EOF)
        if (Ch == '\n')
            ++Counter;
    return(Counter);
}

/* Quick & dirty integer log 10 function, to convert
 * from # of lines to field width for line number
 */
int log10 (int N)
{
    int     L = 1;

    while (N /= 10)
        ++L;
    return(L);
}

/* Copy lines from given file to stdout,
 * with line numbers prepended
 */
void Number_Lines (FILE *fp, int Field_Width)
{
    char    Line[256];
    int     Line_Counter;

    *Line = '\0';   /*in case fscanf fails (blank line)*/
    for (Line_Counter = 1 ;
            fscanf(fp, "%256[^\n]", Line) != EOF ;
        ++Line_Counter) {
        printf("%*d %s\n",
                Field_Width, Line_Counter, Line);
        getc(fp);    /* skip the newline */
        *Line = '\0';   /*in case fscanf fails next time*/
    }
}
```

```
main (int argc, char **argv)
{
    FILE    *fp;
    int     Field_Width;

    if (fp = Get_File(argc, argv))  {
        Field_Width = log10(Count_Lines(fp));
        /* now reset the file pointer to the start of file */
        fseek(fp, 0, 0);
        Number_Lines(fp, Field_Width);
    }
}
```

9.
```
/* Demonstrate fgets, fputs, and sscanf.
 * Reads lines from a file named on the command
 * line.  Removes leading double slash if present,
 * plus white space.  Uses Get_File from exersise 8.
 */
#include <stdio.h>
#define   MAXLINE   256  /* unix maximum for input lines*/

main (int argc, char **argv)
{
    FILE *Get_File (int argc, char **argv);

    char    line[MAXLINE], store[MAXLINE];
    FILE    *ifp = stdin;

    if ((ifp = Get_File(argc, argv)) == NULL)
        exit(1);

    while (fgets(line, MAXLINE, ifp) != NULL)
        if (sscanf(line, " // %[^\n]", store) == 1)  {
            fputs(store, stdout);
            fputs("\n", stdout);
        }
        else
            fputs(line, stdout);
}
```

10.

```
/* Program to print random integers to a file */
#include <stdio.h>

/* Ask user for # of numbers and output file name */
void get_info (char *file_name, int *n_ptr)
{
    printf("\n%s\n\n%s",
        "This program creates a file of random numbers.",
        "How many random numbers would you like?  ");
    scanf("%d", n_ptr);
    printf("\nIn what file would you like them?  ");
    scanf("%s", file_name);
}

/* careful file open for write -
 * warns user if file already exists
 */
FILE *cfopen (char *file_name, char *mode)
{
    char    reply[2];
    FILE    *gfopen(char *, char *), *fp;

    if (strcmp(mode, "w") == 0
            && (fp = fopen(file_name, "r")) != NULL)  {
        fclose(fp);
        printf("\nFile exists.  Overwrite it? ");
        scanf("%1s", reply);
        if (*reply != 'y' && *reply != 'Y')  {
            printf("\nBye!\n\n");
            exit(1);
        }
    }
    fp = gfopen(file_name, mode);
    return fp;
}

/* Write n random numbers to output file */
void prn_rands(int n, FILE *ofp)
{
    int     i;

    for (i = 1 ; i <= n ; ++i)  {
        fprintf(ofp, "%12d", rand() );
        if (i % 6 == 0 || i == n)
            fprintf(ofp, "\n");
    }
}
```

```
/* open a function gracefully; exits if cannot open */
FILE *gfopen (char *fn, char *mode)
{
    FILE    *fp;

    if ((fp = fopen(fn, mode)) == NULL)  {
        fprintf(stderr, "Cannot open %s -- bye!\n", fn);
        exit(1);
    }
    return(fp);
}

main ()
{
    char    file_name[256];
    int     num_rands;
    FILE    *fp;

    get_info(file_name, &num_rands);
    fp = cfopen(file_name, "w");
    prn_rands(num_rands, fp);
}
```

11. We ensure that the digit string is followed only by optional white space by using the control string "%d%c", i.e. read a string of digits, then optional white space, then a scan set consisting only of the newline, with assignment suppression.

```
/* Revised program to print random integers to a file
 * Uses careful read_int function
 */
#include <stdio.h>
#define    MAXLINE    256

/* Read a positive integer.
 * Anything other than a digit string surrounded by
 * optional white space is an error.
 * Re-input on error.
 */
int read_int (FILE *ifp)
{
    char    line[MAXLINE], ch;
    int     error, n;

    do {
        printf("Input a positive integer:  ");
        fgets(line, MAXLINE, ifp);
        error = scsanf(line, "%d%c", &n, &ch) != 2
                          || n <= 0 || !isspace(ch);
        if (error)
            printf("\nERROR: Do it again.\n");
    } while (error);
    return(n);
}

/* Ask user for # of numbers and output file name */
void get_info (char *file_name, int *n_ptr)
{
    printf("\n%s\n\n%s",
        "This program creates a file of random numbers.",
        "How many random numbers would you like?  ");
    *n_ptr = read_int(stdin);
    printf("\nIn what file would you like them?  ");
    scanf("%s", file_name);
}
```

```c
/* careful file open for write -- warns user if file
 * already exists
 */
FILE *cfopen (char *file_name, char *mode)
{
    char    reply[2];
    FILE    *gfopen(char *, char *), *fp;

    if (strcmp(mode, "w") == 0
            && (fp = fopen(file_name, "r")) != NULL)  {
        fclose(fp);
        printf("\nFile exists.  Overwrite it? ");
        scanf("%1s", reply);
        if (*reply != 'y' && *reply != 'Y')  {
            printf("\nBye!\n\n");
            exit(1);
        }
    }
    fp = gfopen(file_name, mode);
    return fp;
}

/* Write n random numbers to output file in a nice format */
void prn_rands(int n, FILE *ofp)
{
    int     i;

    for (i = 1 ; i <= n ; ++i)  {
        fprintf(ofp, "%12d", rand() );
        if (i % 6 == 0 || i == n)
            fprintf(ofp, "\n");
    }
}

/* open a function gracefully; exits if cannot open */
FILE *gfopen (char *fn, char *mode)
{
    FILE    *fp;

    if ((fp = fopen(fn, mode)) == NULL)  {
        fprintf(stderr, "Cannot open %s -- bye!\n", fn);
        exit(1);
    }
    return(fp);
}
```

```
main ()
{
    char    file_name[256];
    int     num_rands;
    FILE    *fp;

    get_info(file_name, &num_rands);
    fp = cfopen(file_name, "w");
    prn_rands(num_rands, fp);
}
```

12.
```
/* Double space a file safely; writes
 * to stdout instead of command line arg
 */
#include <stdio.h>
#include <stdlib.h>

void double_space(FILE *, FILE *);
void prn_info(char *);

main(int argc, char **argv)
{
    FILE    *ifp;

    if (argc != 2)  {
        prn_info(argv[0]);
        exit(1);
    }
    ifp = fopen(argv[1], "r");
    double_space(ifp, stdout);
    fclose(ifp);
}

void double_space (FILE *ifp, FILE *ofp)
{
    int     c;

    while ((c = getc(ifp)) != EOF)  {
        putc(c, ofp);
        if (c == '\n')
            putc('\n', ofp);
    }
}
```

```
void prn_info (char *pgm_name)
{
    printf("\n%s%s%s\n\n%s%s\n\n",
        "Usage:   ", pgm_name, "  infile  > outfile",
        "The contents of infile will be double-spaced ",
        "and written to standard output.");
}
```

13.
```
/* Double space a file safely; writes to
 * stdout instead of command line arg.  Message output
 * written to stderr instead of stdout
 */
#include <stdio.h>
#include <stdlib.h>

void double_space(FILE *, FILE *);
void prn_info(char *);

main(int argc, char **argv)
{
    FILE    *ifp;

    if (argc != 2)  {
        prn_info(argv[0]);
        exit(1);
    }
    ifp = fopen(argv[1], "r");
    double_space(ifp, stdout);
    fclose(ifp);
}

void double_space (FILE *ifp, FILE *ofp)
{
    int    c;

    while ((c = getc(ifp)) != EOF)  {
        putc(c, ofp);
        if (c == '\n')
            putc('\n', ofp);
    }
}

void prn_info (char *pgm_name)
{
    fprintf(stderr, "\n%s%s%s\n\n%s%s\n\n",
        "Usage:   ", pgm_name, "  infile  > outfile",
        "The contents of infile will be double-spaced ",
        "and written to standard output.");
}
```

```
14.    /* Double space a file safely.
        * Writes to stdout instead of command line arg.
        * Error message written to stderr instead of stdout.
        * Accepts command line option -n which causes output
        * to be "strictly" n-spaced if present.
        * The option if present must be before the file name.
        */
       #include <stdio.h>

       void strictly_space (FILE*, FILE*, int);
       void prn_info(char *);

       main(int argc, char **argv)
       {
           FILE   *ifp;
           char *filename;
           int    strict_spacing = 0;

           if (argc == 3)   {
               if (sscanf(argv[1],"-%d",&strict_spacing) != 1) {
                   printf("Unrecognized option: %s\n", argv[1]);
                   exit(1);
               }
               if (strict_spacing > 3 || strict_spacing < 1) {
                   printf("Spacing must be 1, 2, or 3.\n");
                   exit(1);
               }
               filename = argv[2];
           }
           else {
               if (argc != 2)   {
                   prn_info(argv[0]);
                   exit(1);
               }
               filename = argv[1];
           }
           ifp = fopen(filename, "r");
           strictly_space(ifp, stdout, strict_spacing);
           fclose(ifp);
       }
```

```c
/* If the parameter strict_spacing is non-zero, the file
 * is strictly spaced by that number of lines;
 * otherwise it is double spaced.
 * When a newline is read, output is deferred until a
 * character other than a newline is read.
 * Then the required number of newlines are output, in
 * place of the number of newlines input.
 */
void strictly_space (FILE *ifp, FILE *ofp,
                     int strict_spacing)
{
     int    c, i, spaces, newline_pending = 0;

     while ((c = getc(ifp)) != EOF) {
         if (c == '\n')
             ++ newline_pending;
      else {
             if (newline_pending) {
                 /* # of newines to print =
                  * 2 * # read if not strict spacing,
                  * "strict_spacing" if strict.
                  */
                 spaces = (strict_spacing)
                               ? strict_spacing
                                 : 2 * newline_pending;
                 for (i = 0 ; i < spaces ; ++i)
                     putc('\n', ofp);
                 newline_pending = 0;
             }
             putc(c, ofp);
         }
     }
     /* single newline at end of file */
     putc('\n', ofp);
}

void prn_info (char *pgm_name)
{
    fprintf(stderr, "\n%s%s%s\n\n%s\n%s\n\n",
        "Usage: ", pgm_name, " [-n] infile  > outfile",
        "If n = 1 - 3 infile will be strictly spaced.",
        "Otherwise the infile will be double-spaced.");
}
```

15.
```c
/* Read a number of words from an input file,
 * and place them in a string separated by newlines
 */
#include <stdio.h>

/* Read a number of words from ifp, or until end of
 * file.  Returns the number of words actually read.
 * Places words in string separated by newline.
 */
int getwords(FILE *ifp, int k, char *words)
{
    int    i;

    for (i = 0 ;
         i < k && fscanf(ifp, "%s", words) == 1 ;
       ++i) {
      /* advance pointer to overwrite null
       * placed by scanf.
       */
     words += strlen(words);
    /* put separator and advance pointer */
    *words++ = '\n';
    }
    /* restore end of string marker */
    *words = '\0';
    /* return # of words actually read */
    return(i);
}


/* open a function gracefully; exits if cannot open */
FILE *gfopen (char *fn, char *mode)
{
    FILE    *fp;

    if ((fp = fopen(fn, mode)) == NULL)  {
        fprintf(stderr, "Cannot open %s -- bye!\n", fn);
        exit(1);
    }
    return(fp);
}
```

(15. continued)

```
main ()
{
    char    file_name[256], word_string[256];
    int     num_words;

    printf("Program to read words from a file.\n");
    printf("How many reads do you want to read?  ");
    scanf("%d", &num_words);
    printf("Enter file name:  ");
    scanf("%255s", file_name);
    num_words = getwords(gfopen(file_name, "r"),
                num_words, word_string);

    printf("%d %s\n%s\n",
        num_words,
        "words were actually read. Here they are:",
        word_string);
}
```

16.
```c
/* Program to demonstrate writing strings to a file
 */
#include <stdio.h>

/* Write a string into a file, followed by newline */
void putstring (char *s, FILE *ofp)
{
    while (*s)  {
        putc(*s, ofp);
        ++s;
    }
    putc('\n', ofp);
}

main ()
{
    FILE   *ofp;
    char   string[256];

    printf("Program to put strings into a file.\n");
    printf("Enter file name: ");
    scanf("%s", string);
    ofp = fopen(string, "w");
    if (ofp == NULL) {
        printf("Can't open file %s for writing...bye\n",
                string);
        exit(1);
    }
    printf("Enter strings separated by space:\n");

    while (scanf("%s", string) == 1)
        putstring(string, ofp);
    fclose(ofp);
}
```

17.
```c
/* Program to check if three chars can be ungetc-ed
 * from a file. (The ANSI standard only guarantees that
 * one char chan be ungot, but many systems allow more)
 */
#include <stdio.h>

/* graceful file open from text */
FILE *gfopen (char *fn, char *mode);

main ()
{
    char    file_name[256], c1, c2, c3, c1a, c2a, c3a;
    FILE    *ifp;

    printf("Enter a file name and I'll see if I can");
    printf(" unget three characters from it:\n");
    scanf("%s", file_name);
    ifp = gfopen(file_name, "r");

    /* read three chars */
    c1 = getc(ifp);
    c2 = getc(ifp);
    c3 = getc(ifp);

    /* unget them */
    ungetc(c3, ifp);
    ungetc(c2, ifp);
    ungetc(c1, ifp);

    /* get them again */
    c1a = getc(ifp);
    c2a = getc(ifp);
    c3a = getc(ifp);

    /* see if they're the same */
    printf("First three characters read are %c %c %c\n",
                                    c1, c2, c3);
    printf("After ungetting them and re-reading,");
    printf(" we get %c %c %c\n", c1a, c2a, c3a);
    printf("On this system it is ");
    if (c1 != c1a || c2 != c2a || c3 != c3a)
        printf("not ");
    printf("possible to unget three characters.\n");
}
```

18.
```
/* Simple version of "more" program.
 * Displays an input file 20 lines at a time.
 * Lines longer than SCREENWIDTH characters are
 * broken into multiple lines.
 */
#include <stdio.h>
#define   SCREENWIDTH    80
#define   MAXLINES  20

main (int argc, char **argv)
{
    char    line[SCREENWIDTH + 1];
    FILE    *ifp;
    int i;

    if (argc != 2) {
        printf("Usage: %s  filename\n", argv[0]);
        exit(1);
    }
    if ((ifp = fopen(argv[1], "r")) == NULL)  {
        printf("\nCannot open %s\n\n", argv[1]);
        exit(1);
    }
    /* outer loop to display each screenful */
    for (;;)   {
        /* inner loop to read and display each line */
        for (i = 0 ; i < MAXLINES ; ++i)   {
            /* note fgets includes the newline if one
             * found before SCREENWIDTH chars. If
             * SCREENWIDTH characters are read then
             * no newline is in line array but display
             * cursor will wrap around, preserving screen
             * format
             */
            if (fgets(line, SCREENWIDTH, ifp) == NULL)
                exit(1);
            /* use fputs so no extra newline on output */
            fputs(line, stdout);
        }
    printf("\n---More---\n");
    getchar();
    }
}
```

19.
```c
/* Revised version of first "more" program.
 * Displays multiple input files from command line
 * 20 lines at a time.  If an "-n" (where n is an
 * integer) option is encountered on the command
 * line, all subsequent files are displayed with n
 * lines per screenful.  Lines longer than SCREENWIDTH
 * characters are broken into multiple lines.
 */
#include <stdio.h>
#define    SCREENWIDTH    80

/* display one file a screenful at a time */
void display_file (FILE *ifp, int max_lines)
{
    char    line[SCREENWIDTH + 1];
    int     i;

    /* outer loop to display each screenful of file */
    for (;;)   {

        /* inner loop to read and display each line */
        for (i = 0 ; i < max_lines ; ++i)   {
            /* note fgets includes the newline if one
             * found before SCREENWIDTH chars if
             * SCREENWIDTH characters are read then no
             * newline is in line array but display cursor
             * will wrap around, preserving screen format
              */
            if (fgets(line, SCREENWIDTH, ifp) == NULL)
                return;
            /* use fputs so no extra newline on output */
            fputs(line, stdout);
        }

        printf("\n---More---\n");
        getchar();
    }
}
```

```c
main (int argc, char **argv)
{
    FILE    *ifp;
    int max_lines = 20, i;

    if (argc < 2) {
        printf("Usage: %s [-nn] filename filename ...\n",
                                        argv[0]);
        exit(1);
    }

    /* loop to process each argument */
    for (i = 1 ; i < argc ; ++i) {

        /* check for -nn option */
        if (*argv[i] == '-')  {
            if (sscanf(argv[i], "-%d", &max_lines) != 1)
                printf("Unrecognized option:  %s\n",
                                        argv[i]);
        }
        else {

            /* this arg not an option, open file */
            if ((ifp = fopen(argv[1], "r")) == NULL)
                printf("\nCannot open %s\n\n", argv[1]);
            else
                display_file(ifp, max_lines);
        }
    }
}
```

20.
```c
/* Elementary version of grep.
 * Called as:  search  pattern  file_name
 * Prints all lines in file "file_name" containing
 * the substring "pattern".  Uses library function
 * "strstr" to check for substrings.
 */
#include <stdio.h>
#include <string.h>

main (int argc, char **argv)
{
    char   line[MAXLINE], *pattern;
    FILE   *ifp;

    if (argc != 3)  {
       printf("Usage: %s  filename  pattern.\n", argv[0]);
       exit(1);
    }
    if ((ifp = fopen(argv[2], "r")) == NULL) {
       fprintf(stderr, "\nCannot open %s\n\n", argv[2]);
       exit(1);
    }
    pattern = argv[1];
    while (fgets(line, MAXLINE, ifp) != NULL) {
       if (strstr(line, pattern) != NULL)
          printf("%s\n", line);
    }
}
```

21.
```c
/* Revised version of "grep" program,
 * adding "-n" option to print line numbers.
 * Called as:  search  [-n] pattern  file_name
 */
#include <stdio.h>
#include <string.h>
#define   MAXLINE   256

main (int argc, char **argv)
{
    char   line[MAXLINE], *pattern, *filename;
    int  number, line_num;
    FILE   *ifp;

    if (argc != 3 && argc != 4)  {
        printf("Usage: %s  [-n]  pattern  filename.\n",
                    argv[0]);
        exit(1);
    }
    /* check for -n option; following grep, it must
     * be the first command line arg if present.
     */
    if (strcmp(argv[1], "-n") == 0) {
        number = 1; /* flag to indicate line numbering */
        filename = argv[3];
        pattern = argv[2];
    }
    else {
        number = 0;
        filename = argv[2];
        pattern = argv[1];
    }
    if ((ifp = fopen(filename, "r")) == NULL) {
        fprintf(stderr, "\nCannot open %s\n\n", argv[2]);
        exit(1);
    }
    /* read each line in file, counting lines */
    for (line_num = 1;
            fgets(line, MAXLINE - 1, ifp) != NULL;
       ++line_num) {
        /* check each line for pattern */
        if (strstr(line, pattern) != NULL) {
        /* found a match */
        if (number)
            printf("%d ", line_num);
            printf("%s\n", line);
        }
    }
}
```

22. On one MS-DOS system, the output is:

```
A is for apple
---
A is for apple and alphabet pie.
```

You can tell there are more characters in the file by using MS-DOS *dir* command and examining the file size. On a unix system, the output is:

```
A is for apple and alphabet pie.
---
A is for apple and alphabet pie.
```

23. On our system, the output is

```
Hello!
```

The last `printf` is lost.

PROGRAMMING PROJECT 14-1

Purpose: reading and writing external files; command line arguments.

Until now we have been using file redirection with standard input in order to read input from a file into a program. However, as you have probably noticed, this is often inconvenient since standard input then cannot be used for keyboard input. For example, the data base project from the last chapter could not truly be used interactively unless you wanted to type in the card catalog data base each time.

For this assignment you are to modify your program for the card catalog data base to read in the data base from a named external file, and then use standard input for the menu selections as before. The program should first look for the file name as a command line argument. (Command line arguments are described in section 10.6 of the text.) If no command line argument is given, it should prompt for keyboard input for the file name. If an error occurs on opening the file, the program should display an error message and prompt for keyboard entry of a new file name.

The file containing the card catalog is an ordinary text file. It can be created and edited using vi or another text editor. The format of the file is the same as when entering new cards using the "N" menu option, i.e. one string per line, and with no special delimeter between card entries. For example:

A Book On C
Pohl, Ira and Al Kelley
ANSI C programming
643.23
C By Dissection
Pohl, Ira and Al Kelley
traditional C programming
643.20
etc.

CHAPTER 15

SOFTWARE TOOLS

This chapter is somewhat less formal than the previous chapters, and leaves the topic of programming *per se* to the topic of the environment in which the programmer is working. For this reason not all of the software tools described will be available on all systems. The chapter is oriented towards unix, but in many cases similar utilities are available on DOS and other operating systems. The most important topics are:

- *makefiles* and the *make* utility. This is extensively used by people who maintain large software systems for a living. Makefiles can get quite complex; the testbank for this chapter covers only simple uses of makefiles.

- Interfacing with the operating system from within a C program, via the `system` function and the environment variables, will simplify some programming tasks.

- The various options available for C compilers, such as profiling, viewing preprocessor output, and optimizing compiled code.

- The symbolic debugger. As the text describes, the standard unix debugger *dbx* is not the best one available, but there is no standardization for other debuggers. Most students resist investing the time necessary to learn the debugger on their own. If a good debugger is available on your system, they should be encouraged to use it. One of the most common debuggers on DOS systems is the Turbo debugger used with the Turbo C compiler.

TRANSPARENCY MASTERS

Example: executing system commands from within a program
Environment variables
Typical options to the C compiler
Building an object library
Using the profiler
Steps to follow to start using *dbx*
A simple *makefile*
A more complex *makefile*
Some useful options to the compiler
Other useful software tools

229

ANSWERS TO EXERCISES

1.
```
/* Print out all the environment variables */
#include <stdio.h>

main (int argc, char *argv[], char *env[])
{
    int     i;

    for (i = 0 ; env[i] != NULL ; ++i)
        printf("%s\n", env[i]);
}
```

2.
```
/* Program to sort a file in reverse order.
 * It just calls the unix "sort" utility with the
 * "-r" (reverse) option. Prompts the user if no
 * or too many command line arguments typed.
 */
#include <stdio.h>
#include <stdlib.h>

#define   MAXSTRING 100

/* print instructions for the user */
void prn_info (char *pgm_name)
{
    printf("Usage: %s  filename0, pgm_name);
    printf("Sorts the specified file in reverse order");
    printf(" largest to smallest).0);
}

main (int argc, char **argv)
{
    char    command[MAXSTRING];

    if (argc != 2)
        prn_info(argv[0]);
    else {
        sprintf(command, "sort -r %s", argv[1]);
        system(command);
    }
}
```

5. Clearing the screen at the beginning of the program involves simply placing the appropriate `system` call inside `main()`. For unix, it would be:

```
main (int argc, char **argv)
{
        int   n_cols;
        no_yes    u_case;

        system("clear");
        get_options(argc, argv, &n_cols, &u_case);
        mk_cols(n_cols, u_case);
}
```

On our system, if output is redirected, the screen will not be cleared. The *clear* command inserts control characters into the output stream which cause the terminal to clear the screen (control-L is the most common convention). The screen will be cleared if the redirected output is later displayed.

6. On one system, the result of the makefile in the exercise is:

```
Hello!
Thu Oct 17 14:57:53 1991 PDT
Thu Oct 17 14:57:53 1991 PDT
Thu Oct 17 14:57:53 1991 PDT
/usr/cbd/chap15
chap15.ans
makefile
q.15.1.c
q.15.2.c
temp
Goodbye!
```

If a file named *hello* or *date* exists, then the corresponding lines in the makefile will not be executed. For example, if a file *hello* exists, then the line "Hello!" will not appear in the output. If the '@'s are removed, then each command is displayed, in addition to the output generated by the command:

```
echo Hello!
Hello!
date; date; date
Thu Oct 17 14:58:13 1991 PDT
Thu Oct 17 14:58:13 1991 PDT
Thu Oct 17 14:58:13 1991 PDT
pwd; ls
/usr/cbd/chap15
chap15.ans
makefile
q.15.1.c
q.15.2.c
q.15.6.makefil
echo Goodbye!
Goodbye!
```

7. On our system, the makefile produces the following output shown below. Note that there is only one A3.

```
A3
A1
A2
start
```

```
8.    /* Scan output of "fortune" utility for a fortune
      * containing a given phrase. Saves fortune if found
      * in a file and notifies user by e-mail.
      * The phrase cannot extend over more than one line.
      */
     #include <stdio.h>
     #include <stdlib.h>
     #include <string.h>

     #define   MAXSTRING 100
     #define   MAXLINE         256
     #define   MAXTRIES  1000

     main ()
     {
         char   *phrase[MAXLINE];
         void   Find_Fortune(char *);

         printf("%s%s\n",
             "Enter a phrase terminated by newline, ",
             "and I will find a fortune containing it.");
         /* don't put newline in phrase */
         scanf("%256[^\n]", phrase);

     }
```

```c
/* repeatedly execute "fortune",
 * scan output file for given phrase.
 */
void Find_Fortune (char *phrase)
{
    char   command[MAXSTRING],
           message[MAXLINE],
           *user = getenv("USER"),
           line[MAXLINE];
    FILE   *fp;
    int        i;

    for (i = 0 ; i < MAXTRIES ; ++i)  {
        system("/usr/games/fortune > tmp");
        if ((fp = fopen("tmp", "r")) == NULL) {

          /* if we can't read the file we just
           * created, give up
           */
          printf("ERROR, can't open temp file.\n");
            exit(1);
        }

        /* read each line in file, check for phrase */
        while (fgets(line, MAXLINE - 1, fp) != NULL)
          if (strstr(line, phrase) !=NULL) {

          /* found it! */
          sprintf(message, "%s\n%s%s\n\n",
              "Found a fortune!",
              "It was saved in the file tmp.");
          sprintf(command, "echo \"%s\" | mail %s",
                        message, user);
          system(command);
          fclose(fp);
          exit(0);
          }
      fclose(fp);
    }
}
```

9. The pretty printer indents the `else` and the `printf` which follows it further than they were indented. The original indentation was incorrect; the `else` goes with the second `if`, not the first.

CHAPTER 16

FROM C TO C++

C++ is a topic not traditionally covered in introductory C programming classes. C++ adds a few "niceties" not found in C, such as stream input/output, reference parameters, and inline functions, but the primary advantage is the support of *object oriented programming*. This leads to a new level in structured programming, allowing the programmer to define *Abstract Data Types* and to provide a clean separation between the implementation of a data type and its application. One chapter cannot possibly provide a complete description of object-oriented programming techniques, but hopefully the student will be motivated to go on to study C++ in more detail. For this reason, and also beacuse final exams are inevitably looming by this point in the course, no programming projects are included for this chapter.

TRANSPARENCY MASTERS

A first C++ program illustrating stream output
Stream input and inline functions
A class definition for type `string`
Class `string` with overloading of + and `print`
Class `string` with constructor
Class inheritance

ANSWERS TO EXERCISES

1. The following program writes to the screen using stream I/O.

```
// Demonstrate output streams in C++

#include <iostream.h>

main ()
{
    //  First all on one line
    cout << "she sells sea shells by the seashore0;

    // then on three lines
    cout << "she sells\n" << "sea shells\n" <<
        "by the seashore\n\n";

    // finally, in a box
    cout << "+--------------------+\n";
    cout << "|                    |\n";
    cout << "|    she sells       |\n";
    cout << "|    sea shells      |\n";
    cout << "|    by the seashore |\n";
    cout << "|                    |\n";
    cout << "+--------------------+\n";
}
```

2.
```
// convert distances in yards to meters

#include <iostream.h>

main ()
{
    const double yards_to_meters = 1.0936;
    double     yards, meters;

    cout << "Program to convert yards to meters.\n";
    do {
     cout << "Enter distance in yards:   ";
     cin >> yards;
        if (yards > 0)  {
          meters = yards * yards_to_meters;
          cout << yards << " yards equals " <<
                meters << " meteres.\n";
        }
    } while (yards > 0);
}
```

5. The following program will predict your age next year, given no information about you other than your age this year.

```
// Program to compute your age next year,
// given your age this year

#include <iostream.h>

#define   NAMEMAX   40

main ()
{
    char   name[NAMEMAX];
    int    age;

    cout << "Greetings! Please enter your first name:   ";
    cin >> name;
    cout << "Now enter your age:   ";
    cin >> age;
    cout << "\nHello " << name <<
      ", next year you will be " << age + 1 << ".\n";
}
```

6. The following program generates a table of squares, square roots, and cubes.

```
// print a table of squares, square roots, and cubes

#include <iostream.h>
#include <math.h>

#define   TABLELEN  20

main ()
{
    int   n;

    cout << "Integer\t\tSquare\t\tSquare root\tCube\n";
    cout << "---------------------------------------\
-----------------------\n";

    for (n = 1 ; n <= TABLELEN ; ++n)
      cout << n << "\t\t" << n * n << "\t\t"
        << sqrt(n) << "\t\t" << n * n * n << "\n";
}
```

7. The following program shows the use of reference parameters in C++.

```
// Demonstrate exchange funtion using call-by-reference
#include <iostream.h>

void swap (int& i, int& j)
{
    int    temp;

    temp = i;
    i = j;
    j = temp;
}

main ()
{
    int    num1, num2;

    cout << "Enter two integers:   ";
    cin >> num1 >> num2;
    swap(num1, num2);
    cout << "The numbers swapped are " << num1 <<
        " and " << num2 << ".\n";
}
```

8. The code shown causes an error in traditional C because the type of the `sqrt` function is `double`, but `printf` prints it using `%f`. Function prototypes avoid this because the type of the function is known. In C++ the code would be:

```
#include <iostream.h>
#include <math.h>

main ()
{
    cout << "The square root of 2 is " << sqrt(2) << ".\n";
}
```

9. Here is the class definition and reverse function:

```
class string  {
    char s[max_len];
    int  len;
public:
    void assign (const char* st)
        { strcpy(s, st); len = strlen(st); }
    int  length()   { return (len); }
    void print()
        { cout << s << "\nLength: " << len << "\n"; }
    void reverse()
        {   char *head = s, *tail = s + len - 1, temp;
        while (head < tail) {
            temp = *head;
            *head++ = *tail;
            *tail-- = temp;
        }
    }
};
```

10. The following class definition overloads the `print` function:

```
class string  {
    char s[max_len];
    int  len;
public:
    void assign (const char* st)
        { strcpy(s, st); len = strlen(st); }
    int  length()   { return (len); }
    void print()
        { cout << s << "\nLength: " << len << '\n'; }
    void print(int k)   {   char *t = s;
                while (k-- > 0 && *t != '\0')
                    cout << *t++;
                cout << '\n';
            }
};
```

11. The following class definition overloads the * operator:

```
class string  {
    char  s[max_len];
    int   len;
public:
    void assign (const char* st)
        { strcpy(s, st); len = strlen(st); }
    int   length()   { return (len); }
    void print()
        { cout << s << "\nLength: " << len << "\n"; }
    friend string operator * (string& a, int n);
};

string operator * (string& a, int n)   // overload *
{
    string temp;
    char    *source, *dest;
    int     i;

    // initialize destination string
    dest = temp.s;
    temp.len = 0;

    // loop through source n times
    for (i = 0 ; i < n && temp.len < max_len-1 ; ++i) {
        // copy source to tail of destination
        source = a.s;
     while (*source != '\0' && temp.len++ < max_len-1)
            *dest++ = *source++;
    }
    // don't forget to terminate the destination string
    *dest = '\0';
    return temp;
}
```

Transparency
Masters

/ A simple program to display a line of text */*

```
#include <stdio.h>

main ()
{
    printf("she sells sea shells\n");
}
```

Output when this program is run:

```
she sells sea shells
```

```c
#include <stdio.h>

main ()
{
    /* Three variables of type integer are declared: */
    int     inches, feet, fathoms;

    /* the value 7 is assigned to the variable fathoms */
    fathoms = 7;

    /* next fathoms is multiplied by 6 */
    /* and the result is assigned to feet */
    feet = 6 * fathoms;

    /* then the value of feet is multiplied by 12 */
    /* and the result is assigned to inches */
    inches = 12 * feet;

    printf("Wreck of the Hesperus:\n");
    printf("Its depth at sea:\n");
    printf("    %d fathoms\n", fathoms);
    printf("    %d feet\n", feet);
    printf("    %d inches\n", inches);
}
```

Output of the program:

```
Wreck of the Hesperus:
Its depth at sea:
    7 fathoms
    42 feet
    504 inches
```

preprocessing directives

```
main ()
{
```
declarations
statements
```
}
```

printf()	
Conversion character	**How the corresponding argument is printed**
c	as a character
d	as a decimal integer
e	as a floating point number in scientific notation
f	as a floating point number
g	in the e-format or f-format, whichever is shorter
s	as a string

scanf()	
Conversion character	***What characters in the input stream are converted to***
c	to a character
d	to a decimal integer
f	to a floating point number (float)
lf	to a floating point number (double)
Lf	to a floating point number (long double)
s	to a string

/ A simple program demonstrating* scanf */

```c
#include <stdio.h>

main ()
{
    char   first, middle, last;
    int age;

    printf("Input your three initials");
    printf(" and your age:\n");
    scanf("%c%c%c%d",
        &first, &middle, &last, &age);
    printf("\n%s %c.%c.%c.\n%s %d.\n",
        "Greetings",
        first, middle, last,
        "Next year your age will be",
        age+1);
}
```

Sample run with user input shown in boldface:

```
Input your three initials and your age:
CBD 19

Greetings C.B.D.
Next year your age will be 20.
```

```c
/* Sums are computed. */

#include <stdio.h>

main ()
{
    int cnt = 0;
    float  sum = 0.0, x;

    printf("Input some numbers:   ");
    while (scanf("%f", &x) == 1) {
        cnt = cnt + 1;
        sum = sum + x;
    }
    printf("\n%s%5d\n%s%12f\n\n",
        "Count:", cnt,
        "  Sum:", sum);
}
```

Classification of character set

lowercase letters	a b c . . . z
uppercase letters	A B C . . . Z
digits	0 1 2 3 . . . 9
other characters	+ – * / = ( ) { }
	[ ] < > ' " ! @ #
	$ % & _ | ^ ~ .

white space character such as *blank, newline,* and *tab*

The compilation process

_____

C program		
	→	group characters into tokens
	→	translate to target code

/* Read in two integers and print their sum */

```c
#include <stdio.h>

main ()
{
    int      a, b, sum;

    printf("Input two integers:  ");
    scanf("%d %d", &a, &b);
    sum = a + b;
    printf("%d + %d = %d\n",
           a, b, sum);
}
```

```
/*   a comment   */

/*** another comment ***/

/****/

/*
 *   A comment can be written in this
 *   fashion to set it off from the
 *   surrounding code.
 *
 */


/*****************************
 *     If you wish, you can      *
 *     put comments in a box.   *
 *                                            *
 *****************************/
```

Keywords

auto	double	int	struct
break	else	long	switch
case	enum	register	typedef
char	extern	return	union
const	float	short	unsigned
continue	for	signed	void
default	goto	sizeof	volatile
do	if	static	while

Some examples of valid identifiers:

```
k
_id
iamanidentifier2
so_am_i
```

but not:

```
not#me
101_south
-plus
```

Some examples of integer constants:

```
0
77
12345678900
```
(but too large for the machine?)

But not:

```
0123
-49
123.0
```
(this is an octal constant)
(this is a constant expression)
(this is a floating constant)

Some examples of string constants:

```
"a string of text"
" "                              (the null string)
"         "                      (a string of blanks)
"  a = b + c  "                  (nothing is executed)
"  /* this is not a comment */   "
"a string with quotes \" within"
"one backslash \\ is in this string"
```

But not:

```
/*  "this is not a string"  */
"and
neither is this"
```

Operators						Associativity
( )	++ (postfix)	-- (postfix)				left to right
+ (unary)	- (unary)	++ (prefix)	-- (prefix)			right to left
*	/	%				left to right
+	-					left to right
=	+=	-=	*=	/=	etc.	right to left

Declarations and initializations

int a = 1, b = 2, c = 3, d = 4;

Expression	Equivalent expression	Value
a * b / c	(a * b) / c	0
a * b % c + 1	((a * b) % c) + 1	3
++ a * b - c --	((++ a) * b) - (c --)	1
7 - - b * ++ d	7 - ((- b) * (++ d))	17

Assignment Operators

$= \quad += \quad -= \quad *= \quad /= \quad \%= \quad >>= \quad <<= \quad \&= \quad \char`^= \quad |=$

Declarations and initializations

```
int  i = 1, j = 2, k = 3, m = 4;
```

Expression	Equivalent expression	Equivalent expression	Value
i += j + k	i += (j + k)	i = (i + (j + k))	6
j *= k = m + 5	j *= (k = (m + 5))	j = (j * (k = (m + 5)))	18

```c
#include <stdio.h>
#include <stdlib.h>

main ()
{
    int i, n;

    printf("\n%s\n%s",
        "Random integers are printed.",
        "How many do you want?  ");
    scanf("%d", &n);
    for (i = 0 ; i < n ; ++i) {
        if (i % 5 == 0)
        printf("\n");
        printf("%12d", rand());
    }
    printf("\n");
}
```

Sample run of the above program:

```
Random integers are printed.
How many do you want?   11

     16838        5758      10113      17575      31051
     23010        7419      16212       4086       2749
      5627
```

```c
/*
 *      Organization:   SOCRATIC SOLUTIONS
 *      Programmer:     C. B. Dilligent
 *      Date:           19 April 1993
 *
 *      Purpose:        Birthday greetings
 */

#include <stdio.h>

main ()
{
    printf("\nHAPPY BIRTHDAY!\n\n");
}
```

```
#include <stdio.h>

main ()
{
    int     a = 1, b = 2, c = 3;

    x = a + b;
    printf("x = %d\n", x);
}
```

Compiler error messages produced by above program:

```
Error EXMPL_1.C 7: Undefined symbol
    'x' in function main
Warning EXMPL_1.C 9: 'c' is assigned
    a value that is never used
Warning EXMPL_1.C 9: 'b' is assigned
    a value that is never used
```

Relational, Equality, and Logical Operators

Relational operators:

less than:	<
greater than:	>
less than or equal to:	<=
greater than or equal to:	>=

Equality operators:

equal to:	==
not equal to:	!=

Logical operators:

(unary) negation:	!
logical and:	&&
logical or:	||

Operators	Associativity
() ++ (postfix) -- (postfix)	left to right
+ (unary) - (unary) ++ (prefix) -- (prefix)	right to left
* / %	left to right
+ -	left to right
< <= > >=	left to right
== !=	left to right
&&	left to right
||	left to right
?:	right to left
= += -= *= /= etc	right to left
, (comma operator)	left to right

Declarations and initializations

```
int     i = 1, j = 2, k = 3;
double  x = 5.5, y = 7.7;
```

Expression	Equivalent expression	Value
i < j - k	i < (j - k)	0
-i + 5 * j >= k + 1	((-i) + (5 * j)) >= (k + 1)	1
x - y <= j - k - 1	(x - y) <= ((j - k) - 1)	1
x + k + 7 < y / k	((x + k) + 7) < (y / k)	0

Values of:

expr1	expr2	expr1 && expr2	expr1 || expr2
zero	zero	0	0
zero	nonzero	0	1
nonzero	zero	0	1
nonzero	nonzero	1	1

Values of:

expr1	expr2	expr1 && expr2	expr1 || expr2
F	F	F	F
F	T	F	T
T	F	F	T
T	T	T	T

if-statement

```
if   ( expression )

    statement-1

else

    statement-2
```

```
if   (X < Y)

    Min = X;

else

    Min = Y;

printf("Minimum value is %d.\n", Min);
```

```
/* Another kind of nested if statement.
 * This form is not repeatedly indented. */


printf("Enter the time as HH:MM   ");
scanf("%d : %d", &Hour, &Minute);

if   (Hour > 23)
    printf("Hour too large.\n");

else if   (Hour < 0)
    printf("Hour too small.\n");

else if   (Minute > 59)
    printf("Minute too large.\n");

else if   (Minute < 0)
    printf("Minute too small.\n");

else
    InputOK = 1;


/* InputOK is a boolean variable which would be
 * tested elsewhere in the program.  Note that no
 * more than one error message will be printed
 */
```

while-statement

```
while   ( expression )

    statement
```

```
/* Simple while-loop to find number of
 * digits in a number
 */

Digits = 0;
while  (Num > 0)  {
    Num /= 10;
    Digits++;
}
```

for-statement

for   (*expression-1 ; expression-2 ; expression-3*)

   statement

```
for  (I = 1 ; I <= 10 ; I++)
   printf("%d\n", I);
```

Output will be:

```
1
2
3
4
5
6
7
8
9
10
```

/ A nested for-loop to print a pyramid of asterisks */*

```
for  (Row = 1 ; Row <= Height ; Row++)  {

    /* Draw spaces on left of pyramid*/

    for  (Col = 1 ; Col <= Height - Row ; Col++)

        putchar(' ');

    /* Draw body of pyramid */

    for  (Col = 1 ; Col <= Row ; Col++)

        putchar('*');

    putchar('\n');

}
```

do-statement

```
do  {
        statement
        ...
        statement
}  while  ( expression ) ;
```

/* Simple do-loop to skip blanks in input */

```
do  {
    Ch = getchar();
}  while  (Ch == ' ');
```

/* Here Ch will have next non-blank character */

switch-statement

```
switch ( expression ) {
```

```
case constant-expression:
```

statement

statement

```
break;
```

```
case constant-expression:
```

statement

statement

...

```
case constant-expression:
case constant-expression:
```

. . .

```
default:
```

. . .

```
}
```

```c
/* A simple desk calculator using the switch statement */

double   Num, Acc = 0.0;
char Cmd;
do {
    printf("%lf\n* ", Acc);
    scanf("%f %c", &Num, &Cmd);
    switch  (Cmd)  {
    case '+':
        Acc += Num;
        break;

    case '-':
        Acc -= Num;
        break;

    case '*':
        Acc *= Num;
        break;

    case '/':
        Acc /= Num;
        break;

    case 'q':   case 'Q':
        break;

    default:
        printf("Unrecognized command: %c.\n", Cmd);
    }

} while  (Cmd != 'q' && Cmd != 'Q') ;
```

```
type  function_name  ( parameter_list )
{
    declarations

    statements
}
```

```c
#include <stdio.h>
 void prn_message (int k)
{
    int   i;

    printf("Message for you:\n");

    for  (i = 0 ; i < k ; ++i)
        printf("  Have a nice day!\n");
}

main ()
{
    int   n;

    scanf("%d", &n);
    prn_message(n);
}
```

return from a function with no value:

```
return;
```

return a value from a fuction:

```
return expression;
```

```c
#include <stdio.h>

int min (int x, int y)
{
    if (x < y)
        return x;
    else
        return y;
}

main ()
{
    int   j, k, m;

    printf("Input two integers:   ");
    scanf("%d %d", &j, &k);
    m = min(j, k);
    printf("\n%d is the minimum.\n",
           m, j, k);
}
```

Function prototype:

type function_name (parameter type list);

```
#include <stdio.h>

main ()
{
    int    n;

    void  prn_message(int);

    scanf("%d", &n);
    prn_message(n);
}

void prn_message (int k)
{
    ...
```

Top-Down Design

```c
#include <stdio.h>

main ()
{
    void  prn_banner (void);
    void  prn_headings (void);
    void  read_and_prn_data(void);

    prn_banner();
    prn_headings();
    read_and_prn_data();
}

void prn_banner (void)
{
    ...
}

void prn_headings (void)
{
    ...
}

void read_and_prn_data (void)
{
    ...
}
```

```c
main ()
{
    void  prn_instructions (void);
    void  play (int);

    prn_instructions();
    ...
    play(n);
}

void prn_instructions (void)
{
    tell user how to play
}

void play (int n)
{
    int toss (void);
    int     get_call_from_user (void);
    void    report_a_win (int);
    void    report_a_loss (int);
    void    prn_final_report(int,int,int);

  for each play,
            ... = toss();
        get_call_from_user();
        report_a_win(...);
    or report_a_loss(...);
        prn_final_report(...);
}
```

```c
#include <stdio.h>

main    ()
{
    int    n = 3, sum, compute_sum (int);

    printf("%d\n", n);      /* 3 is printed */
    sum = compute_sum(n);
    printf("%d\n", n);      /* 3 is printed */
    printf("%d\n", sum);
}

int compute_sum (int n)
{
    int    sum = 0;

    /* n gets changed here, but not in main () */
    for ( ; n > 0 ; --n)
        sum += n;
    printf("%d\n", n);      /* 0 is printed */
    return sum;
}
```

Some Character Constants and their integer values

Character constants: `'a' 'b' 'c'` ...   `'z'`
Corresponding values: 97   98   99   ...   112

Character constants: `'A' 'B' 'C'` ...   `'Z'`
Corresponding values: 65   66   67   ...   90

Character constants: `'0' '1' '2'` ...   `'9'`
Corresponding values: 48   49   50   ...   57

Character constants: `'&' '*' '+'`
Corresponding values: 38   42   43

Special Characters

Name of character	Written in C	Integer value
alert	\a	7
backslash	\\	97
backspace	\b	8
carriage return	\r	13
double quote	\"	34
formfeed	\f	12
horizontal tab	\t	9
newline	\n	10
null character	\0	0
single quote	\'	39
vertical tab	\v	11

```
printf("%c", 'a');
        /* a is printed */

printf("%c%c%c", 'A', 'B', 'C');
        /* ABC is printed */

printf("%d", 'a');
        /* 97 is printed */

printf("%c", 97);
        /* a is printed */

printf("%c", '\n');
        /* a newline is printed */

printf("%c", '\'');
        /* a ' is printed */
```

/* Capitalize lower case letters and double space */

```c
#include <stdio.h>

main ()
{
    int   c;

    /* get characters, stop at end of file */
    while ((c = getchar() ) != EOF)

        /* test for lower case letter */
        if ('a' <= c && c <= 'z')

            /* print out upper case letter*/
            putchar(c + 'A' - 'a');
        else if (c == '\n')   {

            /* write the newline */
            putchar('\n');
            /* and another one to double space */
            putchar('\n');
        }
        else
            /* otherwise just output the character */
            putchar(c);
}
```

```
#include <ctype.h>
```

Macro	Nonzero (true) is returned if:
`isalpha(c)`	c is a letter
`isupper(c)`	c is an uppercase letter
`islower(c)`	c is a lowercase letter
`isdigit(c)`	c is a digit
`isalnum(c)`	c is a letter or a digit
`isxdigit(c)`	c is a hexadecimal digit
`isspace(c)`	c is a white space character
`ispunct(c)`	c is a punctuation character
`isprint(c)`	c is a printable character
`isgraph(c)`	c is printable, but not a space
`iscntrl(c)`	c is a control character
`isascii(c)`	c is an ASCII code

Function/Macro	Effect
`toupper(c)`	changes c to uppercase
`tolower(c)`	changes c to lowercase
`toascii(c)`	changes c to ASCII code

```
/* Capitalize lowercase letters and double space */
/* Portable version */

#include <stdio.h>
#include <ctype.h>

main ()
{
    int   c;

    while ((c = getchar()) != EOF)
        /* Check for lower case */
        if (islower(c))
            /* Change to upper case */
            putchar(toupper(c));
        else if (c == '\n') {
            putchar('\n');
            putchar('\n');
        }
        else
            putchar(c);
}
```

/ Counting words */*

```c
#include <stdio.h>
#include <ctype.h>

main ()
{
    int   word_cnt = 0;
    int found_next_word (void);

    while (found_next_word() == 1)
        ++ word_cnt;
    printf("Number of words = %d\n\n",
        word_cnt);
}

int found_next_word (void)
{
    int   c;

    while (isspace(c = getchar() ))
        ;
    if (c != EOF) {
        while ((c = getchar()) != EOF
                && ! isspace(c))
            ;
        return 1;
    }
    return 0;
}
```

Some common programming errors

```
/* An integer, not a char, must be used to check
 * for EOF (= -1).  The code below may work on some
 * systems, but not on all
 */


char        c;          /* wrong */

while ((c = getchar()) != EOF)
    putchar(c);


/* A common mistake is to use = instead of ==
/* The code below will assign newline to c,
 * instead of comparing it and so the comparison
 * will test 'true' every time
 */

if  (c = '\n')   {          /* wrong */
    putchar('\n');
    putchar('\n');
}
```

Integral types

`int`	`unsigned`
`long`	`unsigned long`
`short`	`unsigned short`
`char` `unsigned char`	`signed char`

Floating types

`float`   `double`   `long double`

Arithmetic types = Integral types + Floating types

Decimal representation of numbers (used by people)

10753

$$1 \times 10^4 + 0 \times 10^3 + 7 \times 10^2 + 5 \times 10^1 + 3 \times 10^0$$

Binary representation (used by computers)

1100001

$$1 \times 2^6 + 1 \times 2^5 + 0 \times 2^4 + 0 \times 2^3 + 0 \times 2^2 + 0 \times 2^1 + 1 \times 2^0$$

$$= 1 \times 64 + 1 \times 32 + 0 \times 16 + 0 \times 8 + 0 \times 4 + 0 \times 2 + 1 \times 1$$

$$= 64 + 32 + 1$$

$$= 97$$

$$= \text{'a' in ASCII}$$

Floating types

`float`   **Precision: 6 significant digits**

Range: 10^{-38} to 10^{38}

`double`   **Precision: 15 significant digits**

Range: 10^{-308} to 10^{308}

`long double`
                New in ANSI C, not standardized

Exponential ("scientific") notation:

$$314.159\text{e}-2 = 314.159 \times 10^{-2}$$

$$3.14159\text{e}0 = 3.14159 \times 10^{0}$$

$$0.314159\text{e}1 = .314159 \times 10^{1}$$

Math library

`double sqrt (double)`	**square root**
`double exp (double)`	**Raise to the power** *e*
`double log (double)`	**Natural log (log base** *e*)
`double sin (double)`	**Sine**
`double cos (double)`	**Cosine**
`double tan (double)`	**Tangent**
`double pow (double, double)`	
	Raise number to power
`...`	**many others**

```
char c;
short s;
int i;
unsigned u;
float f;
double d;
```

Expression	Type
c + i	int
i + d	double
d + s	double
i + u	unsigned
f + 1.0	double

(1.0 is a double *constant not a* float*)*

```
double compute (double principal,
                double rate,
          int nyears)
{
    int   i;
    doubleamount = principal;

    rate *= 0.01;
    for (1 = 0 ; i < nyears ; ++i)
        amount *= 1.0 + rate ;
    return amount;
}
```

/ Enumeration Types */*

/ The type specifier */*
```
enum day  {sun, mon, tue, wed, thu,
                 fri, sat};
```

/ Decare variables of this enumeration type */*
```
enum day  d1, d2;
```

/ Possible values must come from type specifier */*
```
d1 = tue;
d2 = sun;

if (d1 == d2)
    ...
```

/ typedef can save some typing */*
```
typedef   enum day  day;

day    d1, d2;
```

/* Compute the next day */

```c
enum day {sun, mon, tues, wed, thu,
          fri, sat};

typedef   enum day  day;

day find_next_day (day d)
{
    day next_day;

    switch (d) {
    case sun:
        next_day = mon;
        break;

    case mon:
        next_day = tues;
        break;

    ...

    case sat:
        next_day = sun;
        break;
    }
    return next_day;
}
```

/* Paper, rock, scissors -- header file */

```
enum    p_r_s {paper, rock, scissors,
          game, help, instructions, quit};

enum    outcome  {win, lose, tie, error};

typedef    enum p_r_s    p_r_s;
typedef    enum outcome outcome;

outcome    compare (p_r_s player,
                    p_r_s machine);
void    game_status (int win_cnt,
                        int lost_cnt,
              int tie_cnt);
void    help_for_the_player (void);
void    prn_instructions (void);
p_r_s  selection_by_player (void);
p_r_s  selection_by_machine (void);
```

Value of n	Binary representation	Two's Complement representation (- n)
7	00000000 00000111	11111111 11111001
8	00000000 00001000	11111111 11111000
9	00000000 00001001	11111111 11110111
-7	11111111 11111001	00000000 00000111

Bitwise Operators

Logical operators: (unary) bitwise complement: ~

bitwise and: &

bitwise exclusive or: ^

bitwise inclusive or: |

Shift operators: left shift: <<

right shift: >>

Declarations and initializations:

```
int    a = 3333, b = -7777;
```

Expression	Binary Representation
a	00001101 00000101
b	11100001 10011111
a & b	00000001 00000101
a ^ b	11101100 10011010
a | b	11101101 10011111

Operators

Operators	Associativity
() ++ (postfix) -- (postfix)	left to right
++ (prefix) + (unary) -- (prefix) - (unary) ! ~ sizeof (type) & (address)	right to left
* / %	left to right
+ -	left to right
<< >>	left to right
< <= > >=	left to right
== !=	left to right
&	left to right
^	left to right
|	left to right
&&	left to right
||	left to right
?:	right to left
= += *= <<= >>= etc	right to left
, (comma operator)	left to right

/* Bit print an int expression. */

```c
#include <limits.h>

void bit_print (int a)
{
    int i;
    int n = sizeof(int) * CHAR_BIT;
    int mask = 1 << (n - 1);

    for (i = 1 ; i <= n ; ++i) {
        putchar(((a & mask) == 0)
                        ? '0' : '1');
        a <<= 1;
        if (i % CHAR_BIT == 0 && i < n)
            putchar(' ');
    }
}
```

```
/* Pack 4 bytes into an int */

#include <limits.h>

int pack (char a, char b,
          char c, char d);
{
    int p = a;

    p = (p << CHAR_BIT) | b;
    p = (p << CHAR_BIT) | c;
    p = (p << CHAR_BIT) | d;
    return p;
}
```

/* Unpack a byte from an int */

```
char unpack (int p, int k)
{
    intn = k * CHAR_BIT;
    unsigned mask = 255;

    mask <<= n;
    return ( (p & mask) >> n);
}
```

```
/* two int's and a pointer to an int */
int     a, b, *p;

a = b = 7;

/* p is assigned the address of a */
p = &a;
```

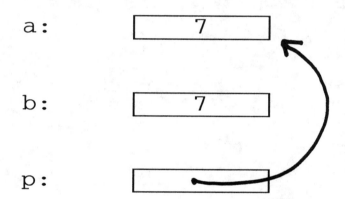

```
/* two int's and a pointer to an int */
int     a, b, *p;

a = b = 7;

/* p is assigned the address of a */
p = &a;

/* Object pointed to by p (i.e. a) gets 3 */
*p = 3;
```

```
/* two int's and a pointer to an int */
int     a, b, *p;

a = b = 7;

/* p is assigned the address of a */
p = &a;

/* Object pointed to by p (i.e. a) gets 3 */
*p = 3;

/* Now p is changed to point to b */
p = &b;
```

a: | 3 |

b: | 7 |

p: | |

```
/* two int's and a pointer to an int */
int     a, b, *p;

a = b = 7;

/* p is assigned the address of a */
p = &a;

/* Object pointed to by p (i.e. a) gets 3 */
*p = 3;

/* Now p is changed to point to b */
p = &b;

/* input integer into address of b */
scanf("%d", p);
```

a: [3   ]

b: [9   ]

p: [   ]

/ swap two integers using call-by-reference */*

```
void swap (int *, int*);

main ()
{
    int a = 3, b = 7;

    /* 3   7 is printed */
    printf("%d  %d\n", a, b);

    /* call swap with addresses of a and b */
    swap(&a, &b);

    /* 7   3 is printed */
    printf("%d  %d\n", a, b);
}
```

/ function parameters declared as pointers */*
```
void swap (int *p, int *q)
{
    int tmp;

    /* use dereferenced pointer to access argument */
    tmp = *p;
    *p = *q;
    *q = tmp;
}
```

```
{
        /* outer block */
        int     a = 2;
        /* 2 is printed */
        printf("%d\n", a);

        {
                /*inner block */
                int     a = 7;
                /* 7 is printed */
                printf("%d\n", a);

                /* back to the outer block */
        }

        /* 3 is printed */
        printf("%d\n", a);
}
```

```
/* external (global) variable declaration and prototype */

int     a = 1, b = 2, c = 3;

int     f(void);

main ()
{
        /* 12 is printed */
        printf("%d\n", f());
        /* 4  2  3 is printed */
        printf("%d  %d  %d\n", a, b, c);
}

int f (void)
{
        int     b, c;   /* b and c are local */
                        /* global b  and  c are masked */

        /* change global a and local b  and  c */
        a = b = c = 4;
        return (a + b + c);
}
```

```
/* register storage class */

{
        register int i;
        /* i will be placed in a high-speed register */
        /* ... if the compiler is able to do so */

        for (i = 0 ; i < LIMIT ; ++i) {
                ...
        }

}        /* block exit will free the register */
```

/* static variables in a function */
/* the variable retains its value between function calls */

```
void f (void)
{
        static int   cnt = 0;

        ++cnt;
        if (cnt % 2 == 0) {
```
/* do something */
```
        }
        else {
```
/* do something different on alternate calls */
```
        }
}
```

/* static external variables are "private" */

```
void f (void)
{
        /* v not available here */
        . . .
}

/* static external variable */
static int   v;

void g (void)
{
        /* v can be used here */
        v = 0;
        . . .
}
```

/ function to count characters and letters */*

```c
int process (int *p, int *nchars_ptr,
                        int *nletters_ptr)
{
    static int   cnt = 0,
         last_char = ' ';

    if (isspace(last_char) &&
        isspace(*p))
      return 0;
    if (isalpha(*p))  {
        ++ * nletters_ptr;
        if (islower(*p))
           *p = toupper(*p);
    }
    else if (isspace(*p))
        if (++cnt % NWORDS ==0)
           *p = '\n';
        else
           *p = ' ';
    ++ * nchars_ptr;
    last_char = *p;
    return 1;
}
```

/* Declare and intialize an array of 8 integers: */

```
int    A[10] = {7, 2, 3, 9, 0, 3, 8, 6};
```

A[0]: | 7 |
A[1]: | 2 |
A[2]: | 3 |
A[3]: | 9 |
A[4]: | 0 |
A[5]: | 3 |
A[6]: | 8 |
A[7]: | 6 |

```c
/* Symbolic definition for size of array: */
#define   N   5

main ()
{
    /* Declaration of array: */
    intA [N],  i,  sum = 0;

    /* Fill the array */
    for (i = 0 ;  i < N ;  ++i)
        A[i] = 7 + i * i;

    /* Print the array */
    for (i = 0 ;  i < N ;  ++i)
        printf("A[%d] = %d ", i, A[i]);

    /* Sum the array's elements */
    for (i = 0 ;  i < N ;  ++i)
        sum += A[i];
    printf("\nsum = %d\n", sum);
}
```

```
/* Count each uppercase letter separately */

main ()
{
    intc, i, letter [26];

    /* initialize the array to zeroes */
    for (i = 0 ; i < 26 ; ++i)
        letter [i] = 0;

    /* count the letters */
    while ( (c = getchar()) != EOF)
        if (isupper(c))
            ++letter[c - 'A'];

    /* print the results */
    for (i = 0 ; i < 26 ; ++i)
        printf("%5c: %4d", 'A' + i,
                        letter[i]);
}
```

```
/* Declare an array and two pointers */
int A[10], *p0, *p1;

/* Set p0 to point to first element of A */
p0 = A;

/* Set p1 to point to second element of A */
p1 = A + 1;
```

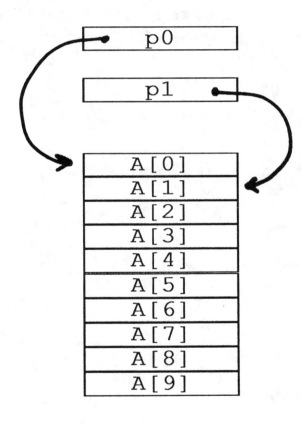

```
/* Summing an array using subscripts */
for (i = 0 ; i < N ; ++i)
    sum += A[i];

/* Summing an array using pointers */
for (p = A ; p < &A[N] ; ++p)
    sum += *p;

/* Summing an array using array variable as a pointer */
for (i = 0 ; i < N ; ++i)
    sum += *(A + i);

/* Summing an array using pointer with subscripts */
p = A;
for (i = 0 ; i < N ; ++i)
    sum += p[i];
```

```
/* Function to sum elements of an array
 * Array ID is passed as a pointer
 * Size of array is passed as separate int
 */
int sum (int A[], int size)
{
    int i, s = 0;

    for (i = 0 ; i < n ; ++i)
        sum += A[i];
    return s;
}
```

Various ways that **sum()** *might be called*

Invocation	*What gets computed and returned*
`sum(v, 100)`	`v[0] + v[1] + ... + v[99]`
`sum(v, 88)`	`v[0] + v[1] + ... + v[87]`
`sum(&v[7], k-7)`	`v[7] + v[8] + ... + v[k-1]`
`sum(v+7, 2*k)`	`v[7] + v[8] + ... + v[2*k+6`

/ Bubble sort function */*

```c
void bubble (int A[], int n)
{
    int i, j;

    for (i = 0 ; i < n - 1 ; ++i)
        for (j = n - 1 ; i < j ; --j)
            if (A[j - 1] > A[j])
                swap(&A[j - 1], &A[j]);
}
```

Unordered data:	7	3	66	3	-5	22	-77	2
First pass:	-77	7	3	66	3	-5	22	2
Second pass:	-77	-5	7	3	66	3	2	22
Third pass:	-77	-5	2	7	3	66	3	22
Fourth pass:	-77	-5	2	3	7	3	66	22
Fifth pass:	-77	-5	2	3	3	7	22	66
Sixth pass:	-77	-5	2	3	3	7	22	66
Seventh pass:	-77	-5	2	3	3	7	22	66

/ Declaration of a two-dimensional array: */*
```
int         a [3] [4] ;
```

	col 1	col 2	col 3	col 4
row 1	a[0][0]	a[0][1]	a[0][2]	a[0][3]
row 2	a[1][0]	a[1][1]	a[1][2]	a[1][3]
row 3	a[2][0]	a[2][1]	a[2][2]	a[2][3]

```
#define    NROWS 3
#define    NCOLS 4

main ()
{
    /* Declare a two dimensional array: */
    int a [NROWS] [NCOLS], i, j ;

    /* Fill the array */
    for (i = 0 ; i < NROWS ; ++i)
        for (j = 0 ; j < NCOLS ; ++j)
            a [i] [j] = i + j;

    /* Print array values */
    for (i = 0 ; i < NROWS ; ++i) {
        for (j = 0 ; j < NCOLS ; ++j)
            printf("a [%d] [%d] = %d   ",
                    i, j, a [i] [j]);
        printf("\n');
    }
}
```

Expressions equivalent to a [i] [j]

* (a [i] + j)

(* (a + i)) [j]

* ((* (a + i) + j)

* (& a [0] [0] + 5*i + j)

```
/* Function to sum the elements of a two dimensional array
 * The size of the LAST subscript must be specified
 */
int sum (int a [] [5])
{
    int i, j, s = 0;

    for (i = 0 ; i < 3 ; ++i)
        for (j = 0 ; j < 5 ; ++j)
            s += a [i] [j];
    return s;
}
```

The following parameter declarations are equivalent:

```
int sum (int a [] [5])

int sum (int (*a) [5])

int sum (int a [3] [5])
```

```c
#include <stdio.h>
#include <stdlib.h>      /* needed for calloc */

main ()
{
    int *A, n ;

    /* input the size for the array */
    scanf("%d", &n);

    /* dynamically allocate space for n  int's */
    A = calloc(c, sizeof(int));

    /* use the array */
    ...

    /* free the memory space */
    free(A);
}
```

```
#define    MAXWORD    100
```

/* *A string is stored as an array of characters* */
```
char   W [MAXWORD];
```

/* *The* `%s` **conversion reads a string** */
```
scanf("%s", W);
```

If the input is ABC, *we have:*

The null character \0 *is the end of string sentinel*

```
/* Have a nice day
 * But print the user's name backwards
 */

char   name[100], c;
int i;

printf("Hi! What is your name? ");
for (i = 0 ;
        (c = getchar()) != '\n' ;
        ++i)
   name[i] = c;
name[i] = '\0';

printf("Nice to meet you, %s.\n",
         name);
printf("Your name backwards is:");
for (--i ; i >= 0 ; --i)
   putchar(name[i]);
```

```
/* Declare a string of length 4
 * and initialize it to "abc"
 */
char   s[] = "abc";

/* The initialization below is equivalent */
char   s[] = {'a', 'b', 'c', '\0'};


/* Initializing a pointer is different: */
char   *p = "abc";
```

p: ┌──────────•──────────→ │ a │ │ b │ │ c │ │ \0 │

/ Process a string using pointers */*

```c
char   *change (char *s)
{
    static char  new_string[MAXLINE];
    char   *p = new_string;

    *p++ = '\t'
    for ( ; *s != '\0' ; ++s)
        if (*s == 'e')
            *p++ = 'E';
        else if (*s == ' ') {
            *p++ = '\n';
            *p++ = '\t';
        }
        else
            *p++ = *s;
    *p = '\0';
    return new_string;
}
```

/* Count the number of words in a string */

```c
#include <ctype.h>
int word_cnt (char *s)
{
    int     cnt = 0;

    while (*s != '\0')  {
    /* Skip white space */
    while (isspace(*s))
        ++s;

        if (*s != '\0')  {
        /* Found a word */
        ++cnt;

        /* Skip the word */
        while (!isspace(*s) &&
               *s != '\0')
                ++s;
    }
     }
    return cnt;
}
```

/ Echo the command line arguments */*

```
main (int argc, char *argv[])
{
    int i;

    printf("argc = %d\n", argc);
    for (i = 0 ; i < argc ; ++i)
        printf("argv[%d] = %s\n",
                        i,
                        argv[i]);
}
```

Some string handling functions in the standard library

```
char *strcat (char *s1,
              const char *s2);
```
Appends string s2 **to the end of** s1.

```
int strcmp (const char *s1,
            const char *s2);
```
Compares two strings lexographically.
Returns zero if s1 **equals** s2.
Returns negative if s1 **less than** s2.
Returns positive if s1 **greater than** s2.

```
char *strcpy (char *s1,
              const char *s2);
```
Copies s2 **into** s1.

```
unsigned strlen (const char *s);
```
Returns the number of characters in s.

Declarations and initializations	
```char s1[] = "beautiful big sky country",``` ``` s2[] = "how now brown cow";```	

Expression	Value
`strlen(s1)`	25
`strlen(s2 + 8)`	9
`strcmp(s1, s2)`	*negative integer*
Statements	**What gets printed**
`printf("%s", s1 + 10);`	`big sky country`

`strcpy(s1 + 10, s2 + 8);`
`strcat(s1, "s!");`
`printf("%s", s1);`
	`beautiful brown cows!`

`#include` *<filename>*

Looks for *filename* in system directories such as */usr/include*.

`#include` *"filename"*

Looks for *filename* first in the current directory, then in the system directories.

```
#define  SECS_PER_DAY  (60 * 60 * 24)

     (The preprocessor will replace
     all occurrences of SECS_PER_DAY
     with (60 * 60 * 24).)

#define      ARRAY_SIZE      250
```

Sybolic constants aid:
- **Clarity -- "self-documenting" code**
- **Portability -- only change in one place**
- **Reliability -- actual representation in one place**

```
#define   min(x, y)\
        (((x) < (y)) ? (x) : (y))

m = min(u, v)
```

will be changed by the preprocessor to

```
m = (((u) < (v)) ? (u) : (v))
```

You could also code

```
#define   min4(a, b, c, d) \
        min(min(a, b), min(c, d))
```

```
/* qsort -- a fast sort function in std library */

#include <stdlib.h>

void qsort (void *array,
   /* pointer to array to be sorted, any type */

              size_t n_els,
   /* # of elements in array */

              size_t el_size,
   /* sizeof each element */

              int compare(const void *,
                  const void *)
          );
   /* user supplied function to compare elements */
```

```c
#include <stdlib.h>

#define        N   11

int    cmp (const void *, const void *);
void   fill_array (double *a, int n);
void   prn_array (double *a, int n);

main ()
{
    double a[N];

    fill_array(a, N);
    prn_array(a, N);
    qsort(a, N, sizeof(double), cmp);
    prn_array(a, N);
}

int cmp (const void *vp, const void *vq)
{
    const double     *p = vp;
    const double     *q = vq;
    double    diff   =  *p - *q;

    return ((diff >= 0.0)
            ? ((diff > 0.0) ? -1 : 0)
            : +1);
}
```

```
/* causes debugging statement below to be compiled */
#define        DEBUG 1


/* causes debugging statement below to be skipped */
#define        DEBUG 0


#if    DEBUG
    printf("debug: a = %d\n", a);
#endif
```

```
#define       message_for(a, b)  \
    printf(#a " and " #b\
    ": We love you!\n")

main ()
{
   message_for(Carole, Debra);
}
```

expanded by the preprocessor into:

```
main ()
{
    printf("Carole" " and " "Debra"
    ": We love you!\n");
}
```

The **#** *turns the macro arguments into strings*

Header file for a large program written in several source files It contains macros, type definitions, function prototypes, and further includes used by each source file.

```
#ifndef    MK_COLS_H
#define    MK_COLS_H

#include <ctype.h>
#include <stdio.h>
#include <stdlib.h>
#include <string.h>

#define      MAXWORD          100
#define      N_COLS             3
#define      SCREEN_WIDTH      80

typedef enum no_yes {no, yes} no_yes;

void   get_options (int argc,
                    char **argv,
                    int *n_cols_ptr,
                    no_yes *u_case_ptr);
void   mk_cols (int n_cols,
                no_yes u_case);
void   prn_info (char *pgm_name);

#endif
```

/* Common mistakes using macros */

```
#define     PI = 3.14159;
printf("%f", PI)
```
    expands to:
```
printf("%f", = 3.14159;)
```

```
#define     SQ(x)     x * x
SQ(a + b)
```
    expands to:
```
a + b * a + b
```

```
#define     SQ(x)     (x) * (x)
4 / SQ(2)
```
    expands to:
```
4 / (2) * (2)
```

```
#define     SQ (x)     ((x) * (x))
SQ(7)
```
    expands to:
```
(x)   ((x) * (x))   (7)
```

```c
/* A recursive function */
void count_down (int n)
{
    if (n)  {
        printf("%d !   ", n);
        /* The recursive call */
        count_down(n - 1);
    }
    else
        /* The base case */
        printf("\nBLAST OFF\n");
}

main ()
{
    /* The initial call */
    count_down(10);
}
```

```
/* Compute sums recursively */
int sun (int n)
{
    if (n <= 1)
        return n;
    else
        return n + sum(n - 1);
}
```

Function Call	Value Returned
sum(1)	1
sum(2)	2 + sum(1) **or** 2 + 1
sum(3)	3 + sum(2) **or** 3 + 2 + 1
sum(4)	4 + sum(3) **or** 4 + 3 + 2 + 1

```c
/* Reverse characters between s[j] and s[k] */
void reverse (char *s, int j, int k)
{
    if (j < k) {
        /* Swap two characters */
        swap(&s[j], &s[k]);
        /* Recursive call moves both pointers */
        reverse(s, j + 1, k -1);
    }
    /* Done when two pointers meet each other */
}

void swap (char *p, char *q)
{
    char    temp;

    temp = *p;
    *p = *q;
    *q = temp;
}
```

/ Recursive string length */*

```c
int r_strlen (char *s)
{
    /* Base case is null string */
    if (*s == '\0')
        return 0;
    /* Recursive call is one less character */
    else
        return 1 + r_strlen(s + 1);
}
```

```c
/* Divide and Conquer */
/* The best possible min-max algorithm */
void minmax (int a[], int n,
             int *min_ptr, int *max_ptr)
{
  int     min1, max1, min2, max2;

  if (n == 2)
      /* Base case is size 2 */
      if (a[0] < a[1])  {
          *min_ptr = a[0];
          *max_ptr = a[1];
      }
      else {
          *min_ptr = a[1];
          *max_ptr = a[0];
      }
  else {
      /* Halve array for recursive calls */
      minmax(a, n/2, &min1, &max1);
      minmax(a+n/2, n/2, &min2, &max2);
      /* Reconcile results from recursive calls */
      if (min1 < min2)
          *min_ptr = min1;
      else
          *min_ptr = min2;
      if (max1 < max2)
          *maxptr = max2;
      else
          *maxptr = max1;
  }
}
```

```
/* Recursion errors: */
/* Forgetting the base case */

long factorial (long n)
{
    return  n * factorial(n - 1);
}
```

```
/* Recursion errors: */
/* Incomplete base case test */
long factorial (long n)
{
    if (n == 1)
        return 1;
    else
        return  n * factorial(n - 1);
}

factorial(0);
```

```
/* Recursion errors: */
/* Ambiguous use of decrement operator */
long factorial (long n)
{
    if (n <= 1)
        return  1;
    else
        return  n * factorial(--n);
}
```

```
struct student {
    char    name [10];
    int     student_id;
    char    grade;
}   s1, s2;
```

s1:

name

student_id

grade

s2:

name

student_id

grade

```
struct student {
    char     name [10];
    int      student_id;
    char     grade;
}   s1, s2;

s1.grade = 'A';
s1.student_id = 590017
strcpy(s1.name, "Bushker");
```

name	B u s k e r
student_id	590017
grade	A

Declarations and assignments

```
struct student   temp, *p = &temp;

temp.grade = 'A';
temp.last_name = "Bushker";
temp.student_id = 590017;
```

Expression	Equivalent expression	Conceptual Value
temp.grade	p -> grade	A
temp.last_name	p -> last_name	Bushker
temp.student_id	p -> student_id	590017
(*p).student_id	p -> student_id	590017

Operators	Associativity
`()` `[]` `.` `->` `++` (postfix) `--` (postfix)	left to right
`++` (prefix) `--` (prefix) `+` (unary) `-` (unary) `!` `~` `&` (address) `*` (dereference) `sizeof` (type)	right to left
`*` `/` `%`	left to right
`+` `-`	left to right
`<<` `>>`	left to right
`<` `<=` `>` `>=`	left to right
`==` `!=`	left to right
`&`	left to right
`^`	left to right
`|`	left to right
`&&`	left to right
`||`	left to right
`?:`	right to left
`=` `+=` `-=` `*=` `/=` `%=` `>>=` `<<=` `&=` `^=` `|=`	right to left
`,` (comma operator)	left to right

```
#define       CLASS_SIZE      50
#define       NCOURSES        10

struct student {
    char        *last_name;
    int         student_id;
    char        grade;
};

struct date {
    short       day;
    char        month[10];
    short       year;
};

struct personal {
    char                name [20];
    struct date         birthday;
};

struct student_data {
    struct personal     p;
    int                 student_id;
    char                grade[NCOURSES];
};
```

```
/* Examples of typedef */

typedef     char *     string;

typedef     int     INCHES, FEET, YARDS;

#define     N        3
typedef     double     scalar;
typedef     scalar     vector [N];
typedef     scalar     matrix [N] [N];

typedef     struct student_data
                        student_data;
```

```
struct list {
    int             data;
    struct list     *next;
}  a, b, c;

a.data = 1;
b.data = 2;
c.data = 3;

a.next = &b;
b.next = &c;
c.next = NULL;
```

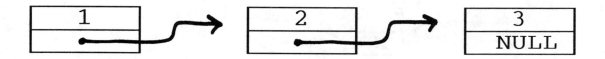

```
typedef     char      DATA;

struct linked_list {
    DATA                    d;
    struct linked_list      *next;
}  head;

typedef   struct linked_list   ELEMENT;
typedef   ELEMENT *            LINK;


head = malloc(sizeof(ELEMENT));
head -> d = 'n';
head -> next = NULL;
```

```
head -> next = malloc(sizeof(ELEMENT));
head -> next -> d = 'e';
head -> next -> next = NULL;
```

```
head -> next -> next =
          malloc(sizeof(ELEMENT));
head -> next -> next -> d = 'w';
head -> next -> next -> next = NULL;
```

/* List creation by recursion */

```c
LINK string_to_list (char s[])
{
    LINK     head;

    /* Base case: empty list */
    if (s[0] == '\0')
        return NULL;
    else  {
        head = malloc(sizeof(ELEMENT));
        head -> d = s[0];
        /* Recursive call */
        head -> next =
            string_to_list(s + 1);
        return head;
    }
}
```

List insertion

Before:

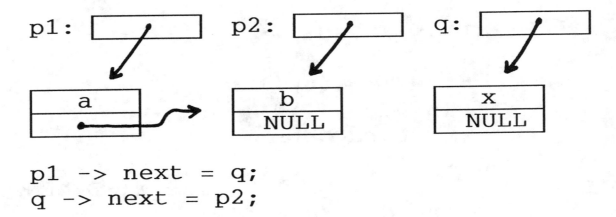

```
p1 -> next = q;
q -> next = p2;
```

After:

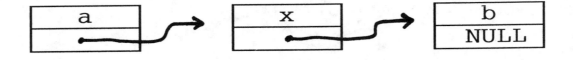

List deletion

Before:

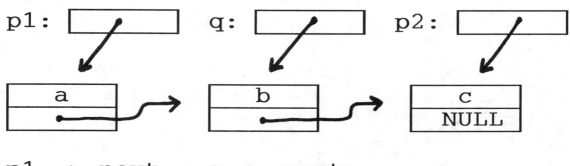

```
p1 -> next = q -> next;
free(q);
```

After:

```
printf()
```

Conversion character	How the corresponding argument is printed
c	as a character
d, i	as a decimal integer
u	as an unsigned decimal integer
o	as an unsigned octal integer
x, X	as an unsigned hexadecimal integer
e	as a floating point number; example: `7.123000e+00`
E	as a floating point number, example: `7.123000E+00`
f	as a floating point number, example: `7.123000`
g	in the e-format or f-format, whichever is shorter
G	in the E-format or f-format, whichever is shorter
s	as a string
p	the corresponding argument is a pointer to `void`; its value gets printed as a hexadecimal number
n	the corresponding argument is a pointer to an integer into which gets printed the number of characters written so far; the argument is not converted
%	with the format `%%` a single `%` is written to the output stream; there is no corresponding argument to be converted

Declarations and initializations

```
int     i = 123;
double  x = 0.12345789;
```

Format	Corresponding argument	How it is printed in its field	Remarks
%d	i	"123"	field width 3 by default
%05d	i	"00123"	padded with zeros
%7o	i	" 173"	right-adjusted, octal
%-9x	i	"7b "	left-adjusted, hexadecimal
%-#9x	i	"0x7b "	left-adjusted, hexadecimal
%10.5f	x	" 0.12346"	field width 10, precision 5
%-12.5e	x	"1.23457e-01 "	left-adjusted, e-format

## Chapter 14

Declarations and initializations

```
char c = 'A', s[] = "Blue moon!";
```

Format	Corresponding argument	How it is printed in its field	Remarks
%c	c	"A"	field width 1 by default
%2c	c	" A"	field width 2, right-adjusted
%-3c	c	"A "	field width 3, left-adjusted
%s	s	"Blue moon!"	field width 10 by default
%3s	s	"Blue moon!"	more space needed
%.6s	s	"Blue m"	precision 6
%-11.8s	s	"Blue moo "	precision 8, left-adjusted

`scanf()`

Unmodified conversion character	Characters in the input stream that are matched	Type of the corresponding argument
c	any character, including white space	char *
d	an optionally signed decimal integer	int *
i	an optionally signed decimal, octal, or hexadecimal integer such as 77 or 077 or 0x77	int *
u	an optionally signed decimal integer	unsigned *
o	an optionally signed octal integer, leading 0 not needed	unsigned *
x, X	an optionally signed hexadecimal integer, leading 0x or 0X not allowed	unsigned *
e, E, f, g, G	an optionally signed floating point number	float *
s	a sequence of nonwhite space characters	char *
p	what is produced by %p in printf(), usually an unsigned hexadecimal integer	void **
n, %, [...]	(See the next table.)	

`scanf()`

Unmodified conversion character	Remarks
n	No characters in the input stream are matched. The corresponding argument is a pointer to `int`, into which gets printed the number of characters read so far.
%	The conversion specification `%%` causes a single `%` character in the input stream to be matched. There is no corresponding argument.
[...]	The set of characters inside the brackets `[ ]` is called the *scan set*. It determines what gets matched and read in. (See the explanation given below.) The corresponding argument is a pointer to the base of an array of characters that is large enough to hold the characters that are matched, along with a terminating null character `\0` that gets appended automatically.

scanf()

Directive in control string	Type of the corresponding argument	What is in the input stream	Remarks
ab%2c	char *	abacus	ab gets matched, ac gets converted
%3hd	short *	-7733	-77 gets converted
%4li	long *	+0x66	+0x6 gets converted (hexadecimal)
-%2u	unsigned *	-123	- gets matched, 12 gets converted
+%lu	unsigned long *	+-123	+ gets matched, -123 gets converted
+%lu	unsigned long *	+-123	+ gets matched, -123 gets converted
+%lu	unsigned long *	+- 123	+ gets matched, error, - cannot be converted
%3e	float *	+7e-2	+7e gets converted
%4f	float *	7e+22	7e+2 gets converted
%5lf	double *	-1.2345	-1.23 gets converted
%4Lf	long double *	12345	1234 gets converted
%p	void **	system-dependent	can read in what printf() writes on output

```
FILE    *ifp, *ofp;
```

/* *Open file for reading* */
/* `my_file` *is the external file name* */
/* *After opening* `ifp` *is used to access the file* */
```
ifp = fopen ("my_file", "r");
if (ifp == NULL)
```
  ERROR*, cannot open file for reading*

/* *Open file for writing* */
```
ofp = fopen ("outfile", "w");
if (ofp == NULL)
```
  ERROR*, cannot open file for writing*

/* Copy a file double-spaced */

```c
void  double_space (FILE *, FILE*);

main (int argc, char **argv)
{
    FILE   *ifp, *ofp;

    ifp = fopen(argv[1], "r");
    ofp = fopen(argv[2], "w");
    double_space(ifp, ofp);
    fclose(ifp);
    fclose(ofp);
}

void double_space (FILE *ifp,
                     FILE *ofp)
{
    intc;

    while ((c = getc(ifp)) ! EOF)  {
        putc(c, ofp);
        if (c == '\n')
            putc('\n', ofp);
    }
}
```

/* Write a file backwards */

/* use binary mode for random access for MS-DOS */
```
ifp = fopen(file name, "rb");
```

/* move to the end of the file */
```
fseek(ifp, 0, 2);
```

/* back up one character */
```
fseek(ifp, -1, 1);
```

/* repeat until at beginning of file */
```
while (ftell(ifp) >= 0) {

    /* move ahead one character */
    c = getc(ifp);
    putchar(c);

    /* back up two characters */
    fseek(ifp, -2, 1);
}
```

```
char    command[MAXSTRING],
        *tmp_file_name;
int     c
FILE    *ifp;
```

/* Create a temporary file name */
```
tmp_file_name = tmpnam(NULL);
```

/* Construct a dir system command */
```
sprintf(command, "dir > %s", tmp_file_name);
```

/* Do the dir, redirecting output to temp file */
```
system(command);
```

/* Now read file containing directory listing */
```
ifp = fopen(tmp_file_name, "r");
```

```
/* Read the environment variables */
main (int arc, char *argv[],
        char *env[])
{
  int i;

  for (i = 0 ; env[i] != NULL ; ++i)
    printf("%s\n", env[i]);
}
```

```
/* Access a particular environment variable */
#include <stdlib.h>

char * getenv (const char * name) ;
```

```
# Makefile for compare_sorts.
# After execution, use prof
# to get a profile

BASE        =   /c/c/blufox
CC          =   gcc
CFLAGS      =   -p
EFILE       =   $(BASE)/bin/compare_sorts
INCLS       =   -I$(BASE)/include
LIBS        =   $(BASE)/lib/g_lib.a

OBJS        =   main.o   chk_arrays.o   ...
$(EFILE):   $(OBJS)
  @echo "linking..."
  @$(CC) $(CFLAGS) -o $(EFILE) $(OBJS) $(L

$(OBJS):   compare_sorts.h
  $(CC) $(CFLAGS) $(INCLS) -c $*.c
```

Building an object library:

First compile the source files into object files.
```
gcc -c gfopen.c gfclose.c
```

Then build the library using unix "ar" utility.
```
ar ruv g_lib.a gfopen.o gfclose.o
ranlib g_lib.a
```

Now the library can be used in compiling a program:
```
gcc -o pgm  *.c  g_lib.a
```

Getting an execution profile

First compile with the "-p" option:
```
gcc -p -o compare_sorts main.c \
    chk_arrays.c ... g_lib.a
```

Then run the program, creating the file *mon.out*:
```
compare_sorts
```

Now run the profiler
```
prof compare_sorts
```

```
%time  cumsecs   #call  ms/call        name
 96.6     2.84       1  2839.00  _slow_sort
  1.4     2.88   11291     0.00    _compare
  1.4     2.92       1    40.00      _qsort
  0.7     2.94       1    20.00       _main
  0.0     2.94       1     0.00    __doprnt
  0.0     2.94       2     0.00     _calloc
  0.0     2.94       1     0.00_chk_arrays
  0.0     2.94       1     0.00       _exit
```

Where was most of the execution time spent?

Steps to follow to start using *dbx*

1 Go to a directory containing a C program.

2 Compile the program with the −*g* option (for debugging).

3 Give the command *dbx pgm*, where *pgm* is the name of the executable file. This invokes *dbx*. From now on, the commands we give are *dbx* commands.

4 Give a command such as *file main.c*. This sets the current file for *dbx*.

5 Give the command *list* to see the first 10 lines in the file. Give the command again to see the next 10 lines.

6 Give the command *stop at n*, where *n* is the line number of an executable line.

7 Give the command you would normally give to invoke *pgm*, except replace the word *pgm* with the word *run*. Example: *run 3*

8 At this point you can step through the program with the commands *step* and *next*. Use *step* to step into functions; use *next* to step over them. Use the command *print var* to print the current value of the variable *var*.

9 Give the command *quit* to quit.

A simple makefile:

```
sum:    main.o    sum.o
    cc  -o sum  main.o  sum.o

main.o:    main.c   main.h
    cc  -c  main.c

sum.o:    sum.c    sum.h
    cc  -c  sum.c
```

"Dependency tree" for previous makefile:

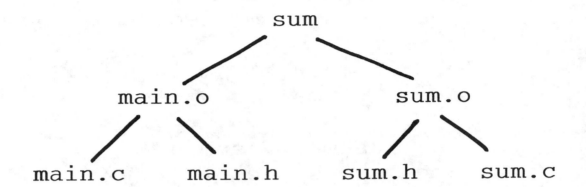

Some useful options to the compiler

-c	Compile only, generate corresponding *.o* files.
-g	Generate code suitable for the debugger.
-o *name*	Put executable output code in *name*.
-p	Generate code suitable for the profiler.
-D *name=def*	Place at the top of each *.c* file the line
	`#define` *name def*
-E	Invoke the preprocessor but not the compiler.
-I *dir*	Look for `#include` files in the directory *dir*.
-M	Make a makefile.
-MM	Make a makefile, but do not include any dependencies on the standard header files.
-O	Attempt code optimization.
-S	Generate assembler code in corresponding *.s* files.

Unix software tools for the programmer:

cb	The C beautifier or "pretty printer"
diff	Prints the lines that differ in two files
grep	Searches for a pattern in one or more files
indent	A C "pretty printer" with many options
wc	Counts lines, words, and characters

Other software tools

awk	Pattern scanning and processing language
csh	This shell, like *sh* and *ksh*, is programmable
lex	Generates C code for lexical analysis
sed	Stream editor that takes its commands from a file
yacc	"Yet another compiler-compiler", used to generate C code

// A first C++ program illustrating output

```
#include <iostream.h>

main ()
{
    cout << "C++ is a better C" << '\n';
}
```

```cpp
#include <iostream.h>

// Constant definition for conversion factor
const double m_to_k = 1.609;

// Inline function for miles to kilometers conversion
inline double convert (double mi)
    { return (mi * m_to_k); }

main ()
{
    double     miles;

    do  {
        cout << "Distance in miles: ";

// Stream input:
        cin >> miles;
        cout << "\nDistance is " <<
            convert(miles) << " km.\n";
    }   while (miles > 0);
}
```

// Overloading the operator +

```
#include <string.h>
#include <iostream.h>

const int     max_len = 256;

class string {
  char      s[max_len];
  int       len;

public:
 void assign (const char* st)
   { strcpy(s, st); len = strlen(st); }

 int length ()   { return(len); }

 void print ()
   { count <<s <<"\nLength: "
           << len << "\n";
 }

 friend string operator+
   (const string& a, const string& b);
};
```

```cpp
#include <string.h>
#include <iostream.h>

const int      max_len = 256;

class string {
  char      s[max_len];
  int       len;

public:
  // A constructor to create a new object of this class
  string (int n)
     { s = new char[n + 1]; len = n; }

  void assign (const char* st)
     { strcpy(s, st);
       len = strlen(st);
     }

  int length ()   { return(len); }

  void print ()
     { count <<s << "\nLength:   "
                  << len << "\n"; }

  friend string operator+
     (const string& a, const string& b);
};
```

// A base class from which a
// derived class will be defined:

```cpp
class shape {
protected:
  int     horiz, vert;
  char    title[10];
public:
  shape (char *name, int i, int j)
    { horiz = i; vert = j;
      strcpy(title, name);
    }
  virtual double area ()
    { cout << "default case\n";
      return 0.0;
    }
  void print ()
    { cout << "I am a shape named "
           << title << "\n";
    }
};
```

```
// Class rectange inherits protected
// and private members of class shape

class rectangle:  public shape {
private:
  int     h2, v2;
public:
  rectangle (char *name, int i1,
             int j1, int i2, intj2):
    shape(name, i1, j1)
             { h2 = i2; v2 = j2; }
  double area ()
    { return fabs((horiz - h2) *
                  (vert - v2));
    }
  void print ()
    { cout << "I am a rectangle named"
           << title << "\n";
    }
} ;
```